The Book of
MAGIC

The Book of
MAGIC

Classic tricks of the great professionals

Bruce Smith

Capella

This edition published in 2008 by Arcturus Publishing Limited
26/27 Bickels Yard, 151–153 Bermondsey Street,
London SE1 3HA

In Canada published for Indigo Books
468 King St W,
Suite 500,
Toronto,
Ontario M5V 1L8

ISBN: 978-1-84193-911-7

Printed in Singapore

Editor: Shona Grimbley
Consultant Magicians: Anthony Owen and Marc Paul
Designer: Graham Curd at wda
Illustrator: Colin Woodman

Contents

Contents

If you want to amaze your friends and family by pulling off a range of tricks with playing cards, rope, rings, handkerchiefs, coins and banknotes, then *The Book of Magic* is for you. From "Odd one out" and "Joker's wild" through "The vanishing banknote" and "Hypnotized hanky" to "Buttonhole release" and Cutting a girl in two", we reveal the secrets of the great magicians. And before you can say, "Abracadabra", you'll be putting together an act full of classic tricks. The pages that follow will show you how to perform authentic and entertaining magic effects, with easy-to-follow, step-by-step instructions and illustrations. In addition the book is packed with fascinating tips and amusing bits of patter, plus brief biographies of famous magicians and insights into the history of magic. This book offers such an excellent grounding in the basics of magic that your audience will soon be scratching their heads, wondering just how you did it. This is the essential guide for budding magicians.

Great
Card Tricks

DEALING
POSITION

FAN OF
CARDS

CUTTING
THE PACK

COMPLETING
THE CUT

Effect *A card flies invisibly from one pile to another.*

This trick works automatically. Try it out on a friend, following the instructions carefully.

• •

1 Ask your friend to hold out their hands as in illustration 1 with their knuckles touching the table.

1

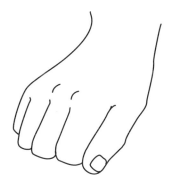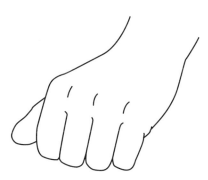

2 From your pack of cards put two cards into each gap between the fingers, except for the last gap, into which you put only ONE card – THE ODD CARD.

3 Starting from the left, remove each pair of cards and split them. Place them separately on the table making two piles (illustration 3).

4 Repeat this with all the pairs – splitting them and adding one card to each pile. Point out that two is an even number.

2   *Put two cards in each gap, except for the last gap.*

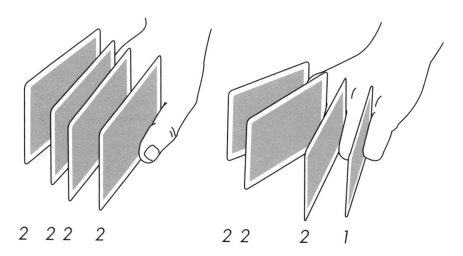

2 2 2 2   2 2   2   1

5 Ask your friend to choose one pile. Explain that you will add the odd card to the pile they choose. When they have selected a pile, bury the odd card somewhere in the middle. Point out that this pile is now odd and the other is even.

6 Replace the cards from the "odd" pile in pairs between the fingers of one hand, as you did originally – amazingly all the cards will be paired up and the odd card has vanished.

> ### *Top tips for tricksters*
>
> *Always practise what you are going to say with your tricks. This is known as the magician's "patter" and should be rehearsed just as carefully as the working and method of the trick.*

3 *Deal the cards into two equal piles.*

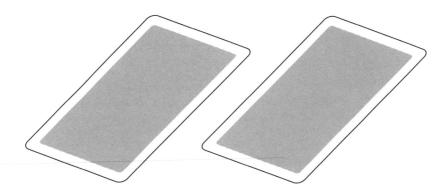

7 Point out that there were an even number of cards. Your friend has two hands, ten fingers, eight gaps between them – all even numbers. The only odd thing in the trick is the one card which seems to have vanished.

8 Replace the "even" pile in pairs between the fingers of the other hand. You will be left with one odd card. It appears as though it has magically jumped across.

Harry Houdini (1874–1926)

Although he later became famous for his daring death-defying escapes, in his early days in show business Houdini was billed as the "King of Kards" (sic).
He would perform sleight-of-hand card tricks similar to the ones described in this book. Even when he was a world famous "escapologist" he would still feature card tricks in his stage performances.

Effect *A spectator has a free choice of four piles of cards. The magician has accurately predicted which pile would be selected.*

Requirements *Write a prediction, as in illustration 2, reading "YOU WILL CHOOSE THE SEVEN PILE". You also need four face-down piles of cards containing i) the four Sevens; ii) any seven odd value cards; iii) two Threes and an Ace; and iv) an Eight, Six, Four and Two.*

● ●

1

2

> # YOU WILL CHOOSE THE SEVEN PILE

1 Ask a spectator to select any one of the four-face down piles. Assure them they can change their mind until they finally settle on one chosen pile.

2 If they choose i), ii), or iii) ask them to read the prediction. You now have an "out" for each pile. If they chose i) show they picked the only pile with the four sevens. If they chose ii) count the cards face down to show it is the only pile containing seven cards. And if they chose iii) show that it is the only pile in which the values add up to seven.

3

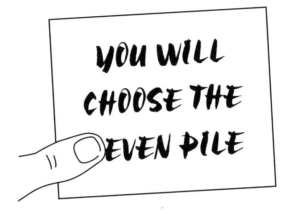

3 If they chose iv) you pick up the prediction and display it – as in illustration 3 – keeping your thumb over the "S" so that it appears to read: "YOU WILL CHOOSE THE EVEN PILE." Show that their selected pile is the only one which contains even cards. Whichever pile they choose it seems as though you knew all along!

Effect *A pile of cards is mixed to a spectator's instructions, but the cards end up in their original order.*

Requirements *For this you will require all 13 cards from one suit.*

Preparation *Set the cards in order Ace through to King as in illustration 1.*

● ●

1 Spread the cards out face up on the table, as in illustration 1, to display the cards in suit order. Now explain to the audience that any casino will tell you that most of the traditional ways that cards are handled aren't particularly secure! Cutting cards does not change the order of the cards and there are many false shuffles to enable you to control the order of the cards while

2

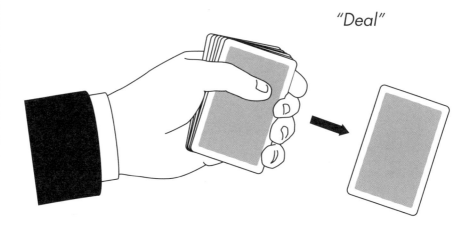

"Deal"

shuffling them. However, there is a method of really mixing cards which you will demonstrate that is called the Duck and Deal.

2 Gather up the pile face down in the dealing position and ask the spectator if they want you to deal or duck the first card. If they say "Deal", simply deal the card face down on the table (illustration 2). If they say "Duck", slide the first card under the second card (illustration 3) and place them both face down on the table (illustration 4).

Top tips for tricksters

Always practise in front of a mirror or a video camera so that you can see exactly how your tricks will look to your audience.

3

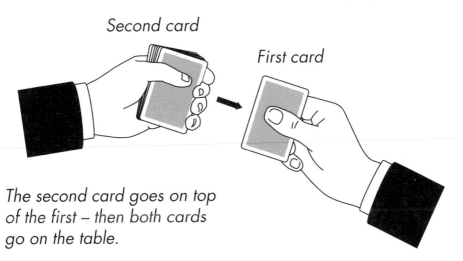

"Duck"

Second card

First card

The second card goes on top
of the first – then both cards
go on the table.

3 Ask the spectator if they want to deal or duck the new top
card of the pile, and continue – following their instructions at
every step – right through the pile. As far as the audience is
concerned it now seems as if the cards have been mixed in a
haphazard way, and you should emphasize that at each step it
is the spectator's choice whether they wish to duck or deal. If you
try this yourself you will be convinced that you have thoroughly

shuffled the cards, but if you go through the pile you will be surprised to discover that in fact the cards are now in reverse order.

4 Collect up the cards from the table, keeping them face down, and repeat the process, going through the pile asking "Duck" or "Deal" with each card. Repeating the action adds to the effect and gives the impression that the cards are thoroughly shuffled.

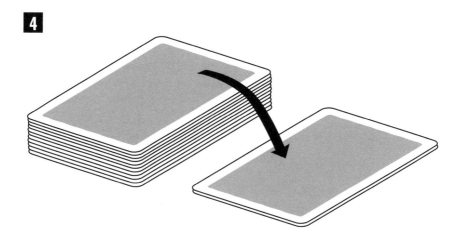

Both top cards go on the table.

In fact what this second process does is to return the cards to the order they were in at the start of the trick.

5 At the end, after following all the spectator's instructions as to whether they want each card ducked or dealt on to the table, you should recap by saying, "The choice throughout has been yours. You have been the magician – I have only been the spectator following your instructions. You would expect the cards to be really mixed up, but as you are the magician please now say a few magic words . . ." (You may find it necessary to suggest a few magic words to them, if they seem at a loss.)

6 After the spectator has said the magic words, deal out the cards face up, one at a time. Deal slowly at first, then get faster and faster. This will increase the drama as the cards are shown to be in the same suit order as they began!

Cardini (1899–1973)

Cardini was the stage name of the Welsh born magician Richard Pitchford. He found fame after he moved to America where he toured the theatres performing an act of flawless card manipulations, apparently plucking fans of cards from thin air. At the height of his fame he returned to London (where he had once been the manager of the magic department in the famous shop Gamages) to star in a Royal Variety Command Performance.

Effect *A message appears magically on the face of the Joker under impossible conditions.*

Requirements *For this you require two identical Jokers, a few extra cards and an elastic band.*

Preparation *Prepare one of the Jokers by writing a suitable message on it as in illustration 1. Add this Joker to the face of the pile and put the elastic band around the whole pile. Cut the other Joker in half and discard the bottom half. The elastic band holds the half Joker in position covering the secret message, so the card appears to the audience as a single complete joker.*

● ●

1

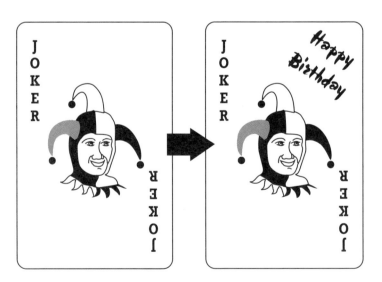

2

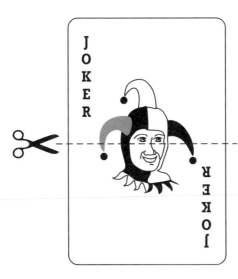

*Cut the second
Joker in half.*

1 Show the Joker on the face of the pile. Tell the audience that the Joker is very clever. In fact, the Joker is actually the most intelligent card in the pack. He has a degree in spelling . . .

2 Turn the pile over and pull the genuine Joker out from under the elastic band (illustration 4). Ensure that you keep the Joker face down. Ask a spectator to keep their hand on top of the Joker. Take the same pen or pencil you used to write on the card and place it under their hand next to the Joker.

Top tips for tricksters

*Never turn your back on an audience
– that's when they might sneak out!*

3 Discard the rest of the pile. Take care that the audience do not see the half Joker on the face of the pile as you place it to one side.

An elastic band holds the half Joker in place.

4 Now turn the Joker face up to show that a message has magically appeared! . . . proving that this really is the world's most intelligent Joker.

5 You can make any suitable message appear on the card. For example, you could have "Happy Birthday", "Congratulations", or the name of your client or your company!

4

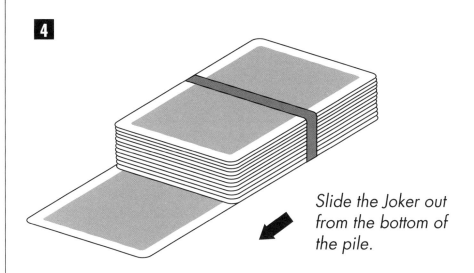

Slide the Joker out from the bottom of the pile.

Dai Vernon (1894–1993)

Dai Vernon is still affectionately remembered by magicians as "The Professor" because of his apparently endless fountain of magical knowledge. Born in Canada, by the age of 12 Vernon had mastered all the sleight-of-hand tricks in the classic book on card handling – The Expert at the Card Table. Vernon fell in love with magic and spent the rest of his life baffling everyone with his ability. At top nightspots in New York he performed his elegant Harlequin Act, which concluded with him filling the stage with live butterflies! He turned down the opportunity to become a famous stage magician and became a lecturer and author on his true love – close-up sleight-of-hand and card magic. He spent the last 30 years of his life in Hollywood, as a mentor for many great close-up magicians. He died aged 98.

♠ Scarlet Pimpernel ♣

They seek him here, they seek him there,
those Frenchies seek him everywhere.
Is he in heaven? Or is he in hell?
That darned elusive Pimpernel.

Effect *The "scarlet" court card vanishes from a pile of three cards.*

Requirements *For this effect you will need three spot cards and one court card.*

Preparation *Cut the court card in half widthways and stick it on to the back of one of the spot cards (illustration 1). Discard the other half of the court card.*

● ●

1 Step the three cards in your left hand, as in illustration 2, so that the half court card is showing in the middle. Explain that the court card represents the famous Scarlet Pimpernel.

2 Pull out the card behind the court card (the Two of Diamonds in illustration 2). Turn it face down and slide it back behind the court card (illustration 3), but slide it square with the centre card. Now turn the pile over.

3 Pull out the face down card which is sticking out (illustration 4). In our effect this is the Two of Hearts. Turn it face up and

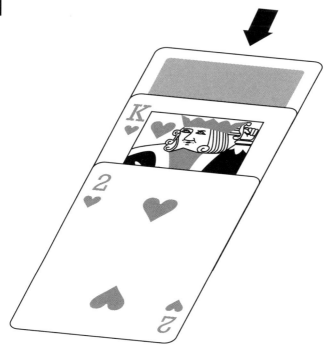

replace it face up behind the other two cards (illustration 5). Turn the pile face down again.

4 Holding the cards in your left hand step the three cards away from you to show three backs as in illustration 6. Ask a spectator to guess which one of the cards is the court card. Most people will select the middle card but it doesn't matter if they don't.

Top tips for tricksters

It is always good to finish with your best trick.

4

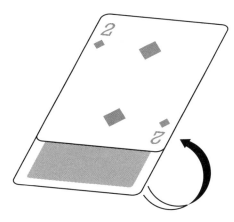

5 Turn over all three cards together (as in illustration 7) to show that all three are spot cards!

5

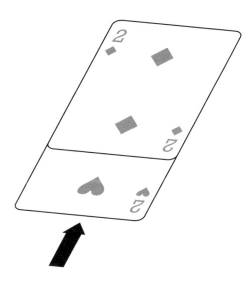

6

6 Deal the cards face up one at a time to show that the Scarlet Pimpernel has escaped once again!

7

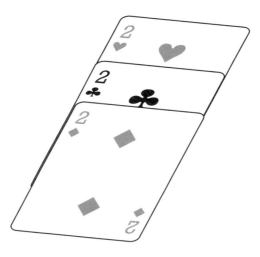

The glide move enables you to secretly substitute one card for another. First we will teach you the move, and then some tricks which use it.

● ●

1 Hold a pile of cards in your left hand in the position shown in illustration 1. This displays the face card to the audience. Notice that your little finger of the left hand is curled around the edge almost touching the face card (the Two of Diamonds in the illustration).

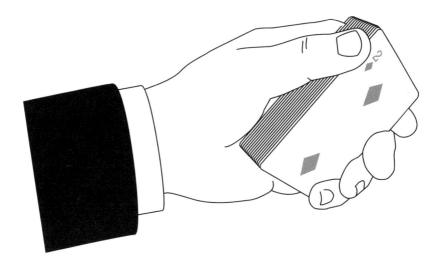

2 Turn your left hand over so that the cards are face down (as in illustration 2). You are apparently going to pull out the face card, that the audience has just seen, from the bottom. In fact you will actually pull out the card second from bottom. This is similar to the move you used for the Queens to Fours trick – but without a hole in the card!

3 Your left little finger contacts the face card and pulls it backwards a little way. Illustration 3 shows this secret movement from underneath.

4 Now it is simple for your right hand to reach under the pile and slide out the card which is one from the bottom (illustration 4).

3

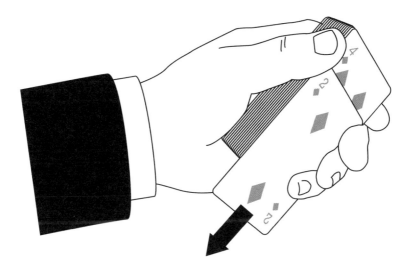

The audience believes this to be the card which they saw on the face a moment before. If you have difficulty pulling back the card with just the little finger you can use the right fingertips to push it back when they reach under to pull out the card.

As you will see in this section there are many great tricks you can do with this move, so it is worth learning and practising it until you can do it perfectly.

Top tips for tricksters

Your audience will be more impressed if you do just one or two tricks really well than several tricks poorly.

4

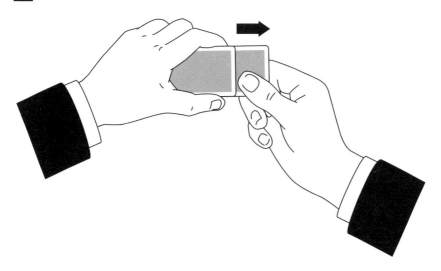

S.W. Erdnase

The Expert at the Card Table *by S.W. Erdnase, first published in 1902, is generally considered to be the card magician's bible. It describes all the major card sleights necessary to cheat at gambling and to perform magic. Yet its author is shrouded in mystery. The book was written under the pseudonym of S.W. Erdnase as the author was a successful card cheat who was revealing the secrets of his dangerous livelihood. But many magicians believe the key to his true identity lies in his name – read backwards it spells Andrews. It is now generally thought that Erdnase was Milton Franklin Andrews, a professional gambler who became famous at the age of 33 – not as a magician, but for shooting three girlfriends and committing suicide. Not all magicians are nice people!*

Effect *The spectator fails an observation test as a card magically changes.*

Requirements *For this you will require the four Kings and one odd card. We have chosen to use an Ace in the description. It is the Ace of Hearts in the illustration.*

Preparation *Set the pile face down with the Ace on top of the four Kings. The spectators must not know how many cards you have.*

• •

1 Hold the pile in the left hand in the face-down glide position. Pull out the first King from the bottom of the pile and place it face up on the table. Pull out the second King and drop that face up on top of the first King.

1

2 Perform the glide on the next card (illustration 1) and, with the right hand, pull out the top two cards squared together as one

2

(illustration 2). This is made easy by the glide. It appears you are just showing another King. Drop the two cards, as one, face up on to the pile on the table (illustration 3).

3 Finally display the last King and drop it face up on top of the pile. Pick up the pile apparently containing just the four Kings and mix the cards, keeping the faces towards you. You need to end up with the Ace in the third position and the King of the same suit on the top of the face-down pile. Challenge the audience to remember the order of the cards. Normally this would be quite simple – but when you shuffle them it becomes almost impossible to know the order.

4 Hold the pile, as you began, in the lefthand face-down glide position. Repeat the actions you did earlier – first card on table, second card on table, glide, double card on table – until you are left with one face-down card in your hand. Ask the audience to guess the suit of each card before you deal it on to the table. If they guess correctly, congratulate them. If they get it wrong, tell them to try harder. Finally you will get to the point where you have just one card left in your hand. Surely they can guess which card it is now, as they can see the other "three" cards face up on the table. The audience believe this to be a King. In fact it is the Ace.

5 Explain that this is an observation test. Which card do they think you are left with? After they have guessed show them that the final King has changed into an Ace. Let them examine the Ace while you scoop up the cards from the table.

3

♠ Cutting the aces ♣

Effect *The spectator cuts the pack into four piles – and the top card of each pile is an Ace!*

Requirements *You require a full pack of 52 cards.*

Preparation *To prepare, secretly set the four Aces face down on top of the pack.*

• •

1 Ask a spectator if they feel lucky. Ask them to cut the face-down pack into four roughly equal piles – A, B, C and D. It is important to keep an eye on the pile that contains the four Aces (pile D).

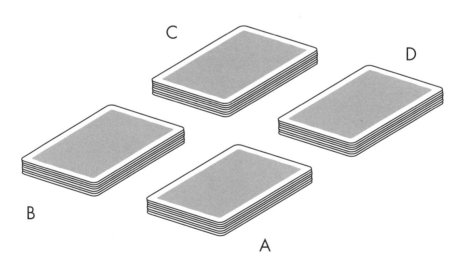

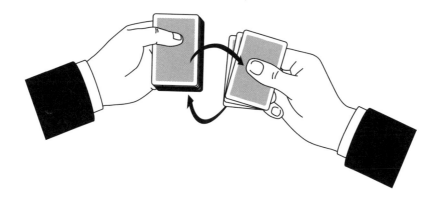

2 Ask the spectator to pick up the first pile (pile A) and move the top three cards from the top of the pile to the bottom (illustration 2). Then ask them to deal a card from the top of pile A on to each of the other three piles (B, C and D). This is shown in illustration 3. Explain that this procedure is to make sure the cards are really thoroughly mixed and the cuts are truly random.

3 Have pile A placed back on the table and repeat the above process with each of the remaining three piles in turn, finishing

> ### Top tips for tricksters
>
> *If a trick goes wrong – don't worry, just move on to your next trick. The audience will only be bothered about it if they think you are!*

3

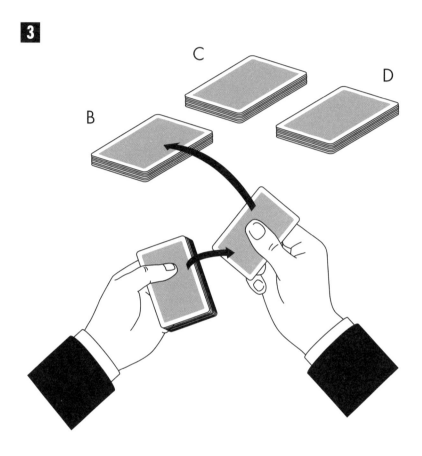

with pile D. Ensure that each pile of cards is replaced in its original position.

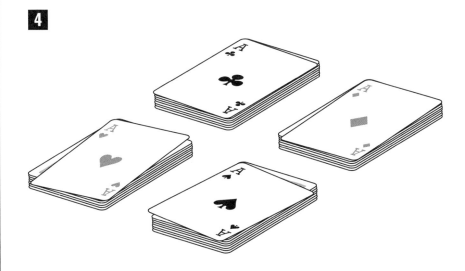

4 When this has been completed with all four piles ask the spectator to turn over the top card of each pile.

They will be amazed to find the four Aces (illustration 4). It must be their lucky day! Suggest that they book their flight for Las Vegas soon!

Nate Leipsig (1873–1939)

Nate Leipsig was a rarity – a vaudeville top-of-the-bill act who had an incredible sleight-of-hand technique. Originally an optician, he became a professional magician and gained a reputation as much for his close-up magic as for his stage performances. He frequently gave stunning performances for royalty and high society, and was very much considered to be the "magician's magician".

Effect *The spectator is able to correctly name a card the magician chooses!*

Requirements *All you need is a full pack of 52 cards.*

Preparation *This requires no secret preparation.*

• •

1 Explain that the spectator is going to do this trick themselves! Ask them to shuffle and mix the cards as much as they like. You now need to select a card. Ask them to fan the cards face towards you. Tell them that you are going to remove a card you have been dreaming about. In actual fact the card you remove is decided by the top two cards of the pack.

1

2 Look at the fan and note the value of the first card and the suit of the second (illustration 1). Now look for the card that matches that combination of suit and value. For example, if the top card is the Four of Clubs and the second card the Queen of Hearts you will look for the Four of Hearts. Remove this card and put it face down to one side. Tell the spectator they now have to discover the name of the card. They will have no idea how to do this, so you offer to help. Explain that they have to work out the suit and the value of the card.

2

3 Ask them to hold the pack face down and deal the cards one at a time face down on to the table to make a single pile (illustration 2). They can stop dealing whenever they wish – the choice is theirs. When they have finished dealing ask them to discard the rest of the pack. They will only need the cards in the pile on the table. These are the cards which will enable them to identify the name of your "dream card".

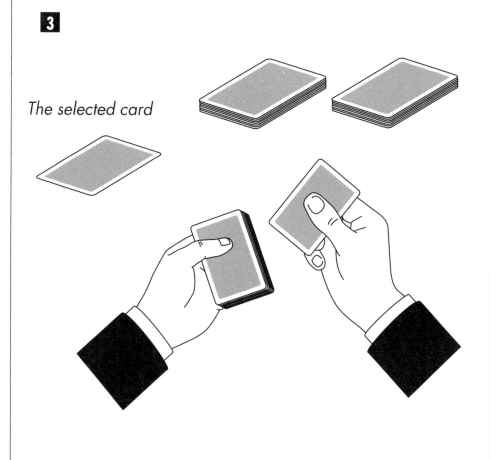

The selected card

4 Explain that your card, like all cards, is made up of two things – a suit and a value. Ask them to pick up the pile of cards and deal them face down into two piles – a suit pile and value pile (illustration 3). They must deal alternately as they would in a game of cards until all the cards from their pile have been used up.

5 Ask them to turn over the top card of each pile (illustration 4). These will be the two cards which began on top of the pack and told you which card to select! One will indicate the suit, the other the value. The spectator can now tell you the name of the card you chose. Turn over your selected card to show they are correct and lead the applause for them! Ask them if there are any other dreams of yours they can tell you about!

4

Effect *A selected card magically appears stuck on the outside of a window!*

Requirements *A full pack of 52 cards, plus an identical duplicate of the card to be "forced".*

Preparation *Before the performance, secretly stick your duplicate card on the outside of a nearby window. For best results use double-sided sticky tape. It is best to stick the card near the corner of the window so that it is slightly covered by the curtain or blinds inside – this will reduce the possibility of anybody noticing the card before your performance. You will be surprised, as I frequently am when I perform this effect, how people do not notice the card stuck on the window. Ensure the force card is on top of the pack.*

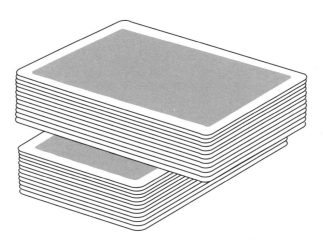

1 Hold the pack face down in your open hand. You are going to perform the classic cross-cut force. Ask a spectator to cut the pack anywhere they like and set their cut cards face down on the table. Drop the cards in your hand on top at right angles to the rest of the pack, creating the cross-cut (illustration 1).

2 Now you talk about the freedom of their selection. In reality the card they cut to is now on top of the pack, but they soon forget this. Lift off the cards you just set on top and hand them the top card of the bottom half. This is actually your force card that began on top of the pack! This is an amazingly deceptive force and requires absolutely no sleight of hand!

3 Now the hard work is done! You ask them to shuffle their card into the pack so that you cannot know its position.

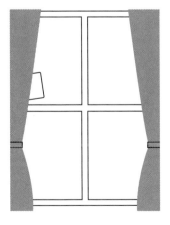

4 When they are happy, throw the pack of cards at the window which has the card stuck on the other side (illustration 2). Watch their amazement as they try to remove their card and discover it is stuck on the outside! This is one of the most powerful tricks in the world of magic – and you will have a lot of fun with it.

Effect *The magician correctly identifies a selected card – first fooling his audience into thinking he has made a mistake.*

Requirements *You need only a full pack of 52 cards.*

Preparation *There is no preparation for this trick.*

• •

1 Ask a spectator to freely select a card from a face-down fan of cards.

2 While your audience are looking at the card secretly glimpse and remember the bottom card of the pack (illustration 1).

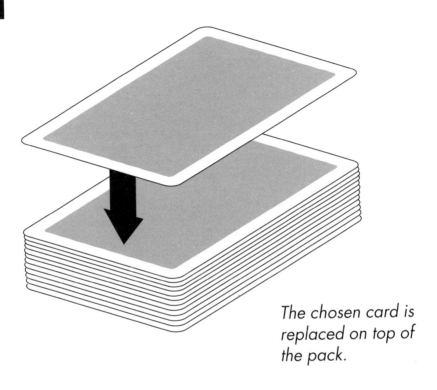

2

The chosen card is replaced on top of the pack.

3 Ask the spectator to replace the card face down on top of the pack (illustration 2). Explain that in a moment you are going to deal through the cards, turning them over one at a time, and you will know instantly exactly which card they selected. If nothing else, the audience should be impressed with your confidence! This bold claim helps to set them up for when the trick appears to go wrong. In fact, you point out, you are so sure you can do it, you might even be willing to bet on it!

4 Ask the spectator to cut the pack and complete the cut. This places your key card next to their selected card.

5 Holding the pack face down in your left hand deal the cards one at a time face up on to the table (illustration 3). The card dealt after your key card will be the selected card, but continue dealing a few more cards on top of this. The audience will assume you have missed the card and got the trick wrong.

Top tips for tricksters

Don't embarrass your volunteers or make them look foolish – they could mess up the trick and make you look even worse!

4

6 Stop dealing and say that you are willing to bet that the next card you turn over will be their card. As they have seen you pass their card they will be enthusiastic to bet. Once you have agreed the stakes reach into the pile of face-up cards, pull out their selected card and turn it face down (illustration 4). If you are the conscientious type you can return their stakes and say that you'll settle for a packet of crisps. If you want to make enemies, then grab the money – and run!

Top tips for tricksters

Always make sure that your fingernails are clean!

Requirements A full pack of 52 cards set up in the order shown in illustration 1.

• •

1 The simplest stack to learn is the one known as the "Si Stebbins" system. The order of the cards is given in illustration 1.

2 By studying illustration 1 you will see how it is always possible to work out what the next card in the sequence will be. Simply add three to the value. Count Jacks as 11, Queens as 12 and Kings as 13. The suits appear in the order of Clubs, Hearts, Spades, Diamonds. You can remember this by thinking of the word CHaSeD, which features the initial letters in order.

3 Set up your pack in the "Si Stebbins" order and familiarize yourself with the system. You can always work out what the card on the top of the pack will be by glimpsing the bottom card. You will be amazed how fast you can get the knack of the system.

4 You are now ready to move on to the other effects in this section.

Top tips for tricksters

Always be sure to give clear instructions to your volunteers to avoid confusion.

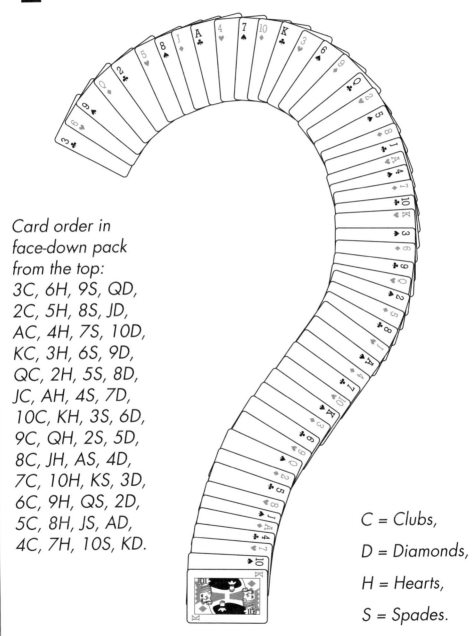

Card order in
face-down pack
from the top:
3C, 6H, 9S, QD,
2C, 5H, 8S, JD,
AC, 4H, 7S, 10D,
KC, 3H, 6S, 9D,
QC, 2H, 5S, 8D,
JC, AH, 4S, 7D,
10C, KH, 3S, 6D,
9C, QH, 2S, 5D,
8C, JH, AS, 4D,
7C, 10H, KS, 3D,
6C, 9H, QS, 2D,
5C, 8H, JS, AD,
4C, 7H, 10S, KD.

C = Clubs,

D = Diamonds,

H = Hearts,

S = Spades.

Effect *The magician deals four hands from a pack of cards. The magician manages to beat three strong hands with a royal flush!*

Requirements *You need a full pack of 52 cards.*

Preparation *Set up the pack in "Si Stebbins" order.*

• •

1 Ask for the pack to be cut – and the cut completed – several times.

2 Take back the cards and cut any Two-value card to the face of the pack. The suit of this card will be the suit of your winning hand (illustration 1).

1

3 Have four hands of five cards each dealt out. Make sure the fourth hand is dealt to you.

4 The first hand will have a strong flush, as will the second and third (illustrations 2, 3 and 4). These are all good betting hands. Ask if anyone would like to make a bet. After all, so far

Top tips for tricksters

It is a good idea to check that your props work okay just prior to a performance, even if they were fine the last time you used them.

3

everything has been carried out as it would be in a real Las Vegas casino – the cards have been freely cut several times and

4

have been correctly dealt out by an impartial dealer (watch out for any bottom or second dealing!). You may find that somebody is willing to gamble – even better!

5 After all the other hands have been revealed slowly turn your cards over, one at a time, to reveal that you have the highest possible hand – the Ten, Jack, Queen, King and Ace all of the same suit – a royal flush! Grab your winnings and head for the door!

5

Effect *A chosen card is torn into quarters and burnt – apart from one corner which is kept back. The card is found restored in the magician's pocket – and the torn corner fits exactly!*

Requirements *You need a full pack of 52 cards and some matches.*

Preparation *Tear a corner off one card – we will assume it is the Joker. Discard the torn corner and set the Joker on the face of the pack as in illustration 1, with the torn section in the bottom lefthand corner.*

• •

1 Spread or fan the cards face down for one to be selected.

2 Keep the squared up pack face down in your left hand (the dealer's grip). Your left fingers will conceal the torn corner of the Joker. Take the selected card (we will assume it is the Five of

Diamonds) and tear off the upper righthand corner. Try to match the tear with that on the Joker. Hand the torn corner of the Five of Diamonds to a spectator for safe keeping.

3 Turn the pack face towards you (be careful that nobody sees that the face card has a torn corner). Hold the pack so that the Joker's torn section is in the bottom left corner. Place the Five of Diamonds on the face of the pack with the torn section in the top right corner. This will cover the tear in the Joker (illustration 2).

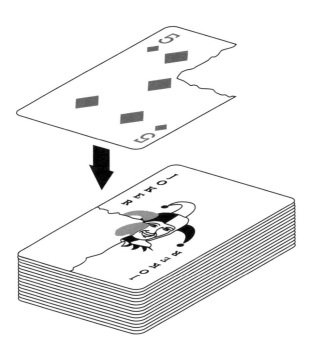

2

3

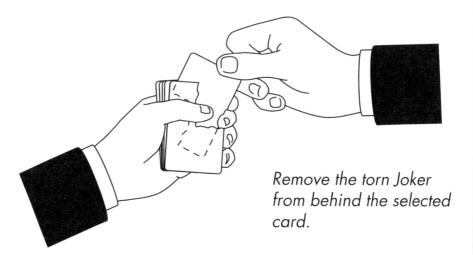

Remove the torn Joker from behind the selected card.

4 You say that you have put the card on the pack so that a spectator can sign their name across the face of the card. When they have done this, you turn the pack face towards you and apparently remove the selected card. In reality you take the duplicate torn card (the Joker). As you can see from illustration 3 this is easy because you just pull it through the gap provided by the torn corner. Keep this card back towards the audience – they must not know this is not the selection. They will assume that it is the selected card because of the torn corner. Place the rest of the pack in an empty pocket.

5 Keeping the card with its back towards the audience, tear it up into little pieces and burn them. When the pieces have all burnt reach into your pocket and pull out the selected card. The corner the spectator has been holding on to fits exactly.

Effect *A selected card penetrates through the centre of a handkerchief.*

Requirements *You need a full pack of 52 cards, plus a thick card and a large opaque handkerchief or headsquare.*

Preparation *Begin with the thick card face down on top of the pack.*

• •

1 Have a card selected and replaced face down on top of the pack, on top of the thick card.

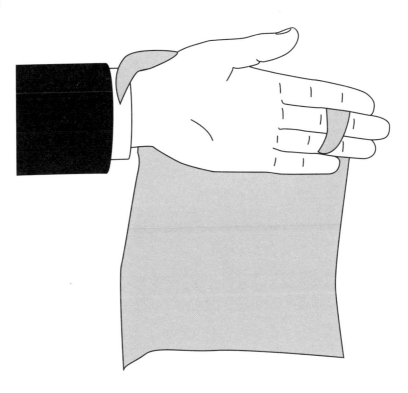

2 Have the cards cut, and complete the cut to lose the selected card in the middle of the pack. The magician now cuts at the thick card. This moves the selected card to the bottom of the pack. Drape the handkerchief over your left wrist (illustration 1), clipping the corner between your fingers so that your thumb is free.

3 Hold the pack in your right hand by one end, keeping the face of the pack towards you. Now you are going to drape the handkerchief over the pack, while secretly taking the selected card in the left hand.

4 As the pack passes behind your left hand, your left thumb peels the selected card from the bottom of the pack and grips it. All this is concealed from your audience by the handkerchief (illustration 2).

2

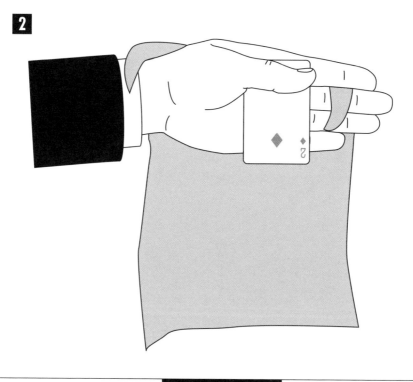

3

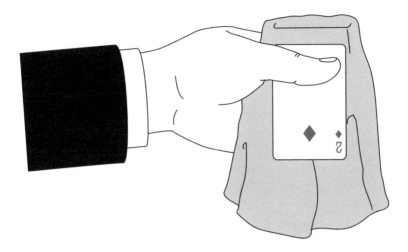

5 Continue moving the pack into the handkerchief and lift it up inside the handkerchief so that it is completely draped. Release the clipped corner of the handkerchief. The card still in your left hand is concealed by the wrapped pack. Move the wrapped pack back towards your left hand and add the concealed card to the outside of the handkerchief (illustration 3).

Top tips for tricksters

The most important rule in producing an act is to remember that audiences will never complain if an act is too short – always leave them wanting more!

4

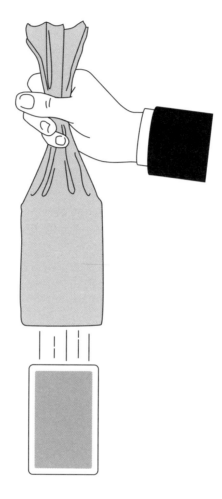

6 Hold the pack through the folds of the handkerchief with the left hand and grab the corners of the handkerchief with the right hand. Shake the handkerchief with the right hand, letting go with the left. The selected card will fall out, apparently penetrating the material (illustration 4).

This section describes two different ways that you can "control" a selected card so that you know its position in the pack. The first control is known as "The Crimp".

• •

1 "The Crimp" is the name for a secret bend in a playing card. The easiest way to secretly put a small bend in a playing card is to hold the pack in your left hand and pull down on the bottom righthand corner of the bottom card with your left little finger to bend it slightly (illustration 1).

1

2 Even if the cards are given a cut you can still find the crimped card in the pack (illustration 2). Make sure that when the crimped card is in the pack you keep the crimped end away from the audience.

3 The gap in the pack created by the Crimp is known as a "Break". You will find it easy to cut to the break, and then cut the crimped card back to the bottom.

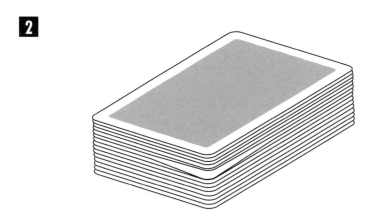

4 To use this control in an effect, ask for a card to be freely selected from the pack. While the audience are noting the card, square up the pack in the left hand and crimp the bottom card of the pack. Have the selected card placed face down on top of the pack. Ask a member of your audience to cut the cards and complete the cut, apparently losing the selected card in the middle of the pack. The selected card is now below the crimped card. So, by cutting to the break you can secretly cut the selection back to the top of the pack. Alternatively, by crimping the top card of the pack you can control the selection to the bottom of the pack.

Effect *A selected card, that is apparently lost in the centre of the pack, adheres to the magician's finger and rises mysteriously out of the pack.*

Requirements *A full pack of 52 cards.*

Preparation *None.*

• •

1 Have a card selected, replaced and control it to the top of the pack (use one of the Basic Card Controls already described).

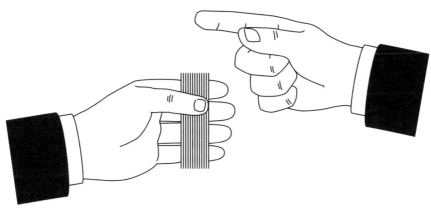

Top tips for tricksters

Practice is perfection dressed in work clothes.

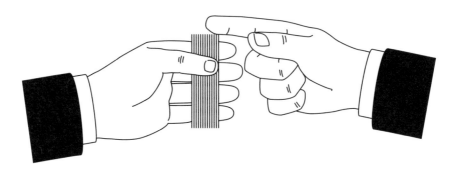

2 Hold the cards in the left hand (illustration 1), with the faces towards your audience.

3 Point your right first finger towards the audience and rub it backwards and forwards across the top short edge of the pack (illustration 2). Explain that you are magnetizing the cards.

4 Hidden behind the pack your right hand secretly extends its little finger (illustration 3).

5 Hold the right hand still and allow the little finger to contact the back of the top card (the selection).

Top tips for tricksters

There is no reward for having talent, only for using it.

6 Slowly lift your right hand straight up about 5cm/2in. Because of your little finger the chosen card will rise up. It will appear to be mysteriously adhering to your right first finger –
it seems that the magical magnetic attraction has worked!

3

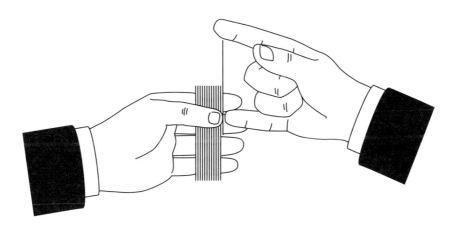

Ken Brooke (1920–1983)

Ken Brooke was a Yorkshireman famed among magicians for his ability to sell them anything. He was what is known as a magical demonstrator, performing the latest tricks which were for sale. At magic conventions and gatherings his stand always had the largest crowds because of his quick wit and charm. He was known especially for his performance of "Chase the Ace" – a version of the Three Card Trick with large playing cards created for use on a big stage.

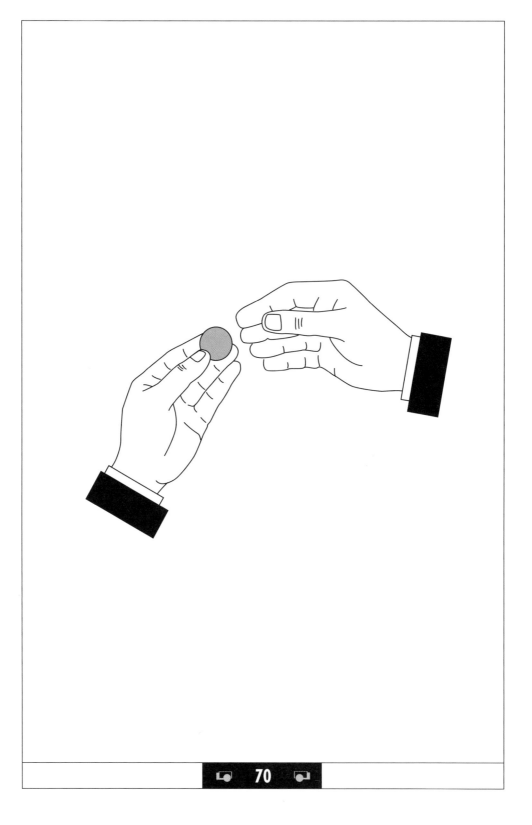

Great Money Tricks

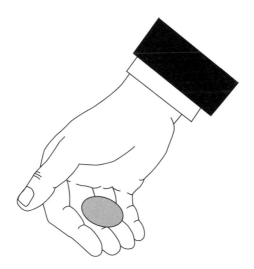

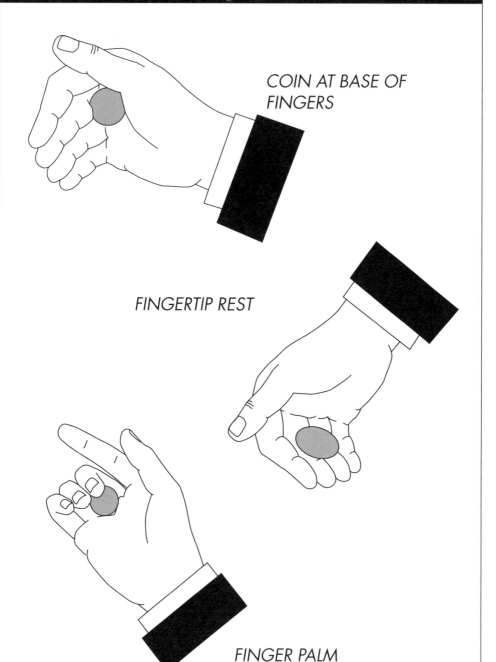

COIN AT BASE OF
FINGERS

FINGERTIP REST

FINGER PALM

Effect *A coin vanishes from the magician's right hand to appear in the left.*

Requirements *Any two coins.*

Preparation *None.*

• •

1 Show a coin on the palm of each hand (illustration 1). The coin in the left hand should be below the third and fourth fingers. The one in the right hand should be at the base of the thumb. Hold the hands 30cm/12in apart on a table top.

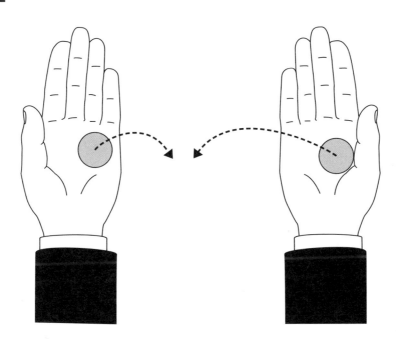

2 At exactly the same time turn both hands over quickly so that the thumbs come close together. As you do this the coin from the right hand will be thrown under the left hand (illustration 2), but to the audience it appears that you have just turned your hands over and there is a coin under each one.

3 Lift your right hand to show that the coin has vanished. Lift the left hand to show that, amazingly, there are now two coins under it.

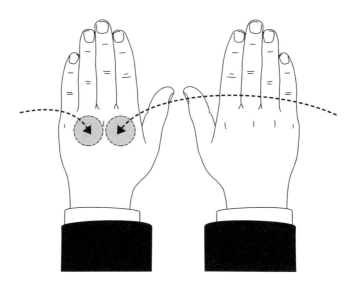

Top tips for tricksters

Money magic is always more effective if the coins or banknotes used in the trick are borrowed from trustworthy members of the audience.

Effect *A banknote is borrowed and rolled up into a tight tube. When it is handed to a member of the audience, the note vanishes. It reappears in the magician's pocket.*

Requirements *A banknote (which you borrow from a member of the audience).*

Preparation *None.*

• •

1 Borrow a banknote from a rich, trusting member of your audience and roll it up into a tight tube.

2 Stand a spectator on your left and hold the banknote tightly in your right hand to stop it unrolling.

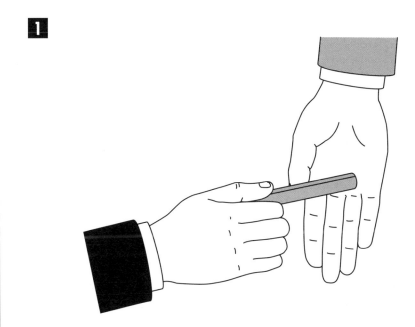

3 Ask the spectator to hold out their right hand palm up. With your left hand hold on to their right wrist.

4 Lift the note up and bring it down to tap the spectator's open hand (illustration 1). Explain that on the count of three the spectator must close their hand around the note.

5 Swing your right hand up in an arc to the right of your face (illustration 2) and back down. Count "one" as the note taps their open hand. Repeat this action and count "two" as you tap their palm again.

6 The next time your hand swings up, you leave the rolled up note tucked behind your ear. The timing must be the same as before – the right hand swings back down as though nothing has happened.

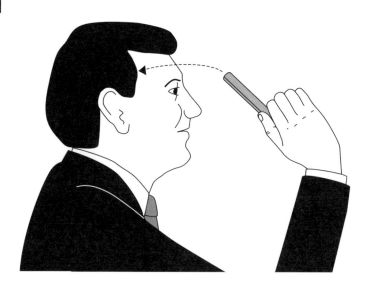

7 Your extended first finger hits the spectator's hand. The spectator will instinctively close their hand around your finger. Ask them to open their hand so that you can have your finger back! This creates an amusing situation for a few moments when it seems that the money has vanished inside the spectator's hand.

8 You can either reveal that the note is tucked behind your right ear or have a duplicate note in your pocket which you can return to your money lender.

The effect makes a great bar bet and stunt, and can be used as a gag or as a strong piece of magic. However, it is not really suitable for a stage presentation.

3

Effect *A coin vanishes.*

Requirements *Any coin.*

Preparation *None.*

● ●

1 Hold the coin horizontally, parallel with the floor, with the tips of your left thumb and fingers. The fingers and thumb should be pointing upwards. Your fingers should be held together so that nobody can see between them.

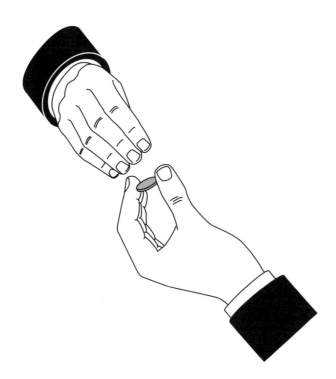

2 Your right hand approaches from behind to apparently pick up the coin (illustration 1). Your right thumb goes under the coin and your right fingers come over the top.

3 As soon as your right fingers cover the coin from view, your left thumb releases the coin, allowing it to fall to the base of your left fingers (illustration 2).

4 However, your right hand continues as though it did contain the coin. It clenches into a fist and moves upwards and away to the right (illustration 3). It is important that you watch the right hand move and hold the left hand still. The rules of misdirection

2

3

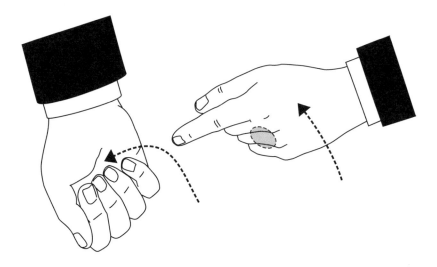

to remember here are first, that the audience will watch a moving object and, second, they will look where you look.

5 Close the left hand, clipping the coin at the base of the left fingers (finger palm position).

6 Open your right hand to show that the coin has vanished!

Top tips for tricksters

It is worthwhile washing your hands before and after you practise as coins can become grubby and dirty very easily.

Effect *A coin vanishes in the magician's hands.*

Requirements *Any coin.*

Preparation *None.*

• •

1 Hold the coin vertically in your left hand, at the tips of your thumb and first three fingers (illustration 1). Keep your fingers tight together so that the audience cannot see between them. The backs of your fingers are towards the audience.

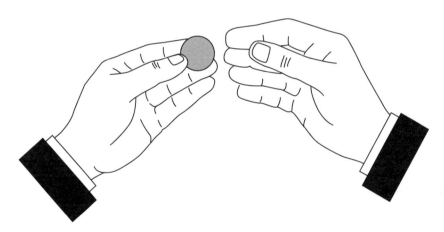

2 The right hand reaches over as though to take the coin from the left hand. The right thumb goes behind the coin and the right fingers cover it at the front.

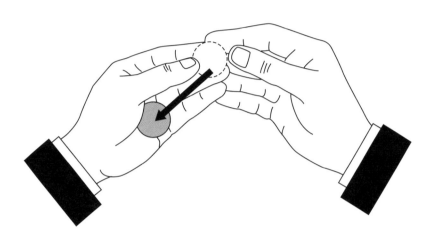

3 As soon as the right fingers completely cover the coin from the audience's view the left thumb releases its hold, and the coin slides down to the base of the left fingers (illustration 2).

David Roth

This New York coin magician is probably today's acknowledged expert at sleight-of-hand magic with coins. Many of his routines are described in detail in the book, David Roth's Expert Coin Magic, written, illustrated and published by Richard Kaufman and available from most good magic shops.

4 The left hand curls slightly to hold the coin in the finger palm position while the right hand moves away to the right, apparently taking the coin (illustration 3).

5 Watch your moving right hand, and allow your left hand to drop naturally to your side. Keep the backs of the right fingers towards the audience so that they do not know the coin is not there (illustration 4).

6 While attention is on your right hand you can secretly slip the coin into your left pocket or keep it finger palmed to be reproduced later.

7 Slowly open the fingers of your right hand to show the coin has vanished!

3

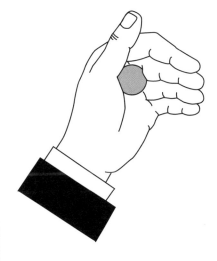 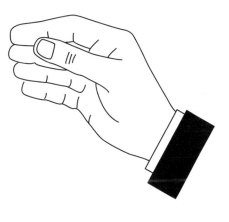

4

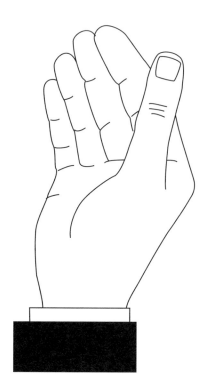

Chung Ling Soo (1861–1918)

One of the highlights of Chung Ling Soo's spectacular show was the "Dream of Wealth". From mid-air he produced coins, banknotes and a cheque for one million pounds! Although known as the Marvellous Chinese Conjurer, the oriental character was actually a disguise for William E. Robinson who was really born in America! He was fatally wounded on stage during a performance of the famous "Catching a Bullet".

Effect *The magician displays at his fingertips a coin of small denomination (for example, a penny). With a magical pass the magician changes it into two coins, both of a much higher value than the original coin!*

Requirements *Three coins (one small and two large).*

Preparation *The two large coins are held upright near the tips of your right thumb and first finger. They are secretly hidden by the smaller coin which you hold upright and at right angles to them, also at the tips of the right thumb and first finger (illustration 1). Hold this set-up in front of a mirror and you will*

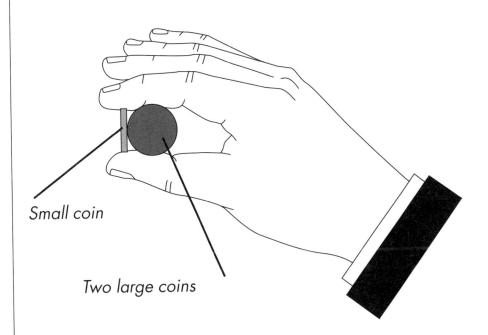

Small coin

Two large coins

see that the two large coins are hidden. Practise the following routine many times in front of a mirror watching it from different angles until you are confident the large coins are completely hidden.

Set up the coins in position and you are ready to begin your performance.

• •

1 Hold up the right hand to show the small coin face on and at the audience's eye level so that they cannot see the two extra coins (illustration 2). The trick will only work if the coin is held at the height of the audience's line of vision. It is important that the edges of the large coins are at the exact centre of the small coin, to give as much cover as possible.

2

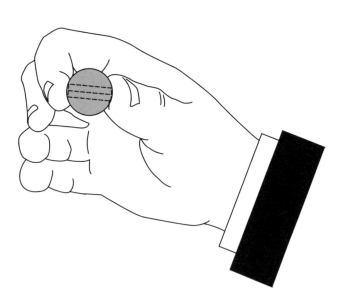

3

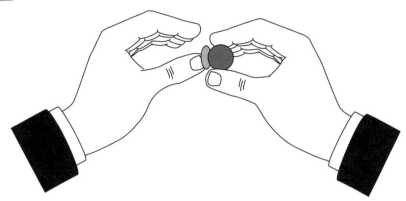

2 The audience have, apparently, seen that your right hand is empty, except for the small coin. Now show both sides of your left hand to prove it is empty.

3 Bring the two hands together with the first fingers and thumbs of both hands pointing towards each other. Again it is essential that the hands stay level with the audience's eye level so they do not see the extra coins.

4 Your left thumb goes beneath the coins, pushing on the bottom edge of the small coin (illustration 3), pivoting it on to the bottom of the two large coins so that all three coins are now in one stack.

Top tips for tricksters

It is a good idea to keep a set of coins especially for performing with. Keep these polished and clean to improve your "professional" image.

5 At the same time tip the three coins forward so that the top coin of the pile (a large coin) faces the spectators head on. The small coin is now hidden at the back of the coin stack (illustration 4).

6 Move your two hands apart; the left hand takes the front coin to the left and the right hand holds the other two coins clipped together and moves them to the right. The small coin is now concealed behind the large coin in the right hand, and held in place by the right thumb.

It will seem that the small coin has grown and doubled in an instant. As you put the coins away be careful not to expose the small hidden coin.

This is a quick visual effect which is ideal for a one-to-one performance, especially when creating extra change at the shop, bank or on the bus!

4

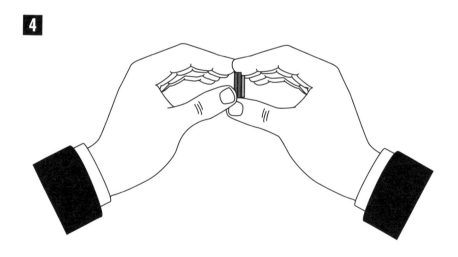

Effect *This is one of the true classics of coin magic, performed by professional magicians all over the world. The magician plucks coins from the air and drops them into a container. In the finale the magician's hands are full of a stream of gleaming coins caught in mid-air.*

Requirements *A special fake coin, a stack of genuine identical coins (about 25), a container (a large tin or a small plastic bucket) and a special holder.*

Preparation *The special coin is made by drilling a hole in a small metal disc the same size as the coins (a blank pet's name tag is ideal for this as it already has the hole in it). Thread a*

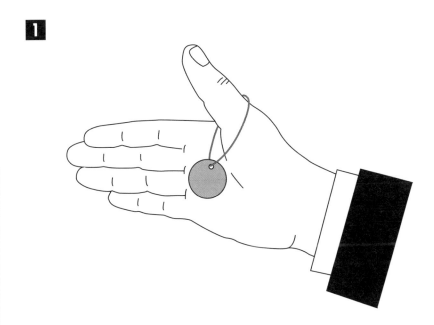

1

small loop of cotton through the hole so that it will loop over your thumb (illustration 1).

The special holder is made from an old sock! This will hold the stack of coins that will make your big final production (about 12). To make the holder cut off the toe of the sock and sew around the edge of the hole with elastic (illustration 2). Put half the coins inside the sock – the elastic should prevent them falling out – and safety pin it under your jacket or coat on your right side.

Your final preparation is to loop the thread on the fake coin over your right thumb and stack the remaining coins (about 12) in your closed left hand. The empty container should be on your table.

All this set-up means that it is best to perform the "Miser's Dream" as an opening effect. It is particularly suitable for this because it is short and noisy!

• •

1 Pick up the container with the right hand and show the audience that it is empty (keeping the special coin hidden in your hand). Pass the container to your left hand which takes it, holding the coins between the left fingers and the inside top edge of the container.

2 Reach forward with the right hand apparently to pluck a coin from the air. Keep the back of the fingers towards the audience to hide the coin dangling from your thumb. Jerk your hand upwards and the coin will flip up to your fingertips – apparently produced in mid-air.

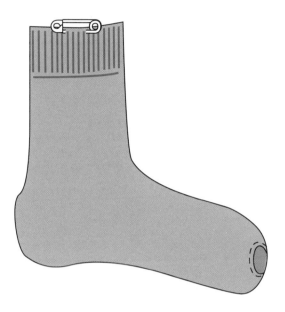

3 Move the right hand to the top of the container and apparently drop the coin inside. What really happens is that you release the coin and it returns to its position dangling around the thumb. At the same time your left fingers allow one coin inside the container to drop to the bottom – the audience will hear it drop. If the timing is right this is very convincing – it seems as though you have just dropped a coin into the container.

Top tips for tricksters

Many fake and gimmicked coins are available from magic shops, dealers and suppliers. You may find a magic shop listed in your local Yellow Pages.

4 By repeating step 2 you can apparently produce another coin! Repeat step 3 and drop it into the container.

5 Continue producing coins until all the coins in your left hand have been dropped into the container. You can produce coins from behind your knee, under your armpit or from your audience! It is a very funny situation to apparently produce coins from behind a spectator's ears, or beard and so on.

6 When the last coin has been dropped, allow your right hand to fall naturally to your side as you shake the container noisily and perhaps jokingly ask if anyone would like to contribute to your collection! While the audience's attention is on the container, your right hand reaches under the right side of your jacket and squeezes the coins out of the holder. Any noise made while you're doing this will be covered by you rattling the container in your left hand.

7 Finally place the container on the table or the floor and open your right hand, letting the final big production of coins stream from your hand into the container (illustration 3). The special coin will fall unnoticed among the regular coins.

Street magicians

Many magicians began their performing lives "on the street" as buskers, trying to extract money from the passers-by. Ex-street magicians enjoying great success today include Harry Anderson, John Lenahan, Keith Fields, Leo Ward and Penn and Teller.

Effect *The magician magically changes four blank pieces of paper into four genuine crisp banknotes!*

Requirements *Four identical banknotes, four blank banknote-sized pieces of paper and some glue.*

Preparation *Hold all the pieces of paper together. Fold in the right and left thirds, then fold the bottom third up and the top third down. Repeat this procedure with the four banknotes.*

Glue the two packages back to back. Then open out the blank sheets. Transfer the top white sheet to the bottom of the pile, covering the banknotes.

• •

1

2

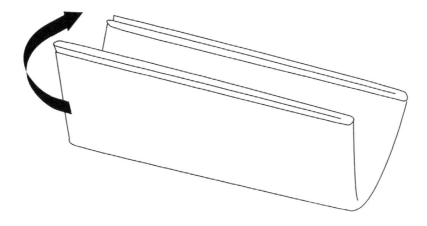

1 Hold the pile of papers in your left hand and show them front and back (illustration 1).

2 Your right hand removes the top sheet and shows it to be blank on both sides.

3 Follow the same procedure and show the second sheet blank both sides.

Coin tricks you can buy

SHELL COIN   This special coin will enable you to perform "Coins Through the Table" or "Coins Across" with ease.

4 Do not show the third sheet – it has a bundle of banknotes stuck on the back!

5 Remove the bottom sheet and show both sides of it before replacing it back ON TOP of the pile.

6 The pile should be held so that everybody is looking down on it – so that the banknotes stuck underneath are concealed (illustration 3).

7 Fold the papers into a package along the creased lines you made earlier (illustration 2).

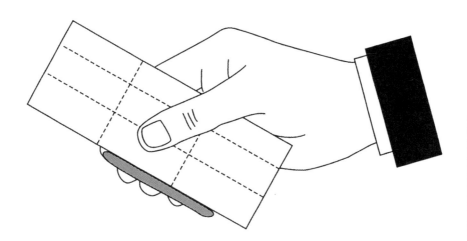

Coin tricks you can buy

COPPER SANDWICH This is a more expensive gimmicked coin box which will enable you to perform more impressive effects.

8 Turn the package over (illustration 4) and open it to show that the blank paper has turned into banknotes. Move the top note to the bottom of the pile and repeat steps 1 to 5 to show they are genuine notes. Then fold them up and stick them in your wallet!

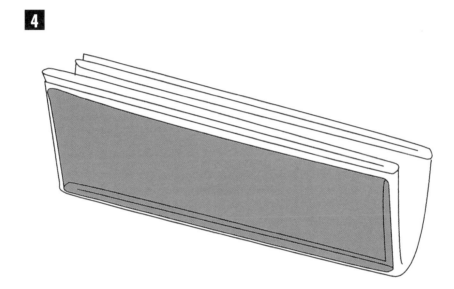

The magic castle

The Magic Castle in Hollywood is considered by many to be the international home for magic. This large Victorian mansion up in the Hollywood hills (not far from the world famous sign) opened its doors as a private magic club in 1963. Only the many thousands of proud members and their guests are allowed to eat in the magical restaurant, watch the nightly magic shows and even see the Castle's piano-playing ghost!

Effect *The magician places a coin in the left fist. When he slaps the back of the fist with his right hand, the coin appears on top of his fist, having apparently penetrated his hand!*

Requirements *Any coin.*

Preparation *None.*

● ●

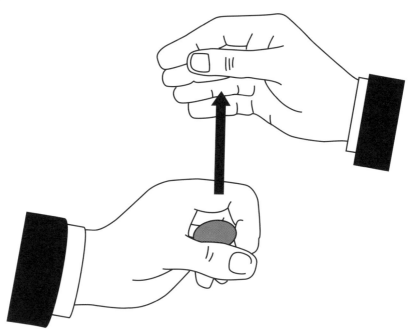

2

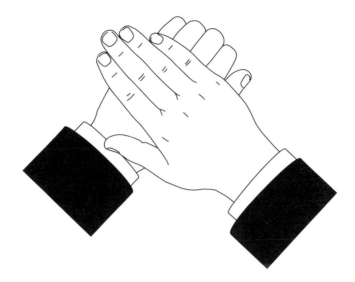

This is a quick visual stunt which looks like clever sleight of hand, but relies more on a special knack which will only take a few minutes to learn. It is not suitable for a big show, but it is fun to do for a few friends with a borrowed coin.

1 Place the coin in your left hand. Close the hand around it in a loose fist, turned palm down.

2 You now appear to simply slap the back of the left hand with the right. As you do this, jerk both hands up slightly and release the coin from the left fist (illustration 1).

3 The coin will fly out of the left fist, hit the right palm and land on the back of the left hand. The right hand then slaps the back of the left, holding the coin in place (illustration 2).

4 Lift the right hand off the left fist to show that the coin has apparently penetrated the hand and landed on the back of the left hand (illustration 3).

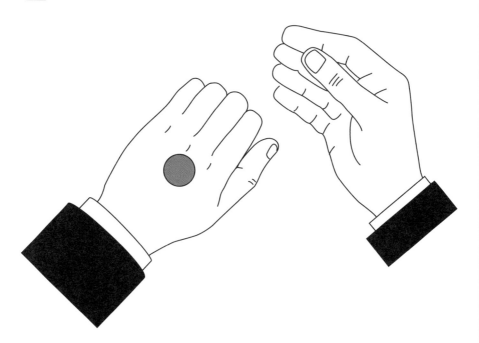

3

Professor Hoffmann (1839–1919)

Professor Hoffmann was the pen-name of Angelo Lewis, a professional barrister and journalist, who was Britain's leading magical author. The first coin tricks to be described in detail appeared in his books. His books are now rarities, sought by magical collectors everywhere, and include Modern Magic, More Magic, Later Magic *and* Magical Titbits.

Effect *Two notes of different denominations are placed on the table, one on top of the other. Magically, they penetrate through each other.*

Requirements *Any two banknotes (preferably borrowed). The only requirement is that they must be of different values or currency so that they can be told apart.*

Preparation *None.*

• •

1 Lay the two notes on the table to form a V. The point of the V is towards you. The lower note is angled away to your left and

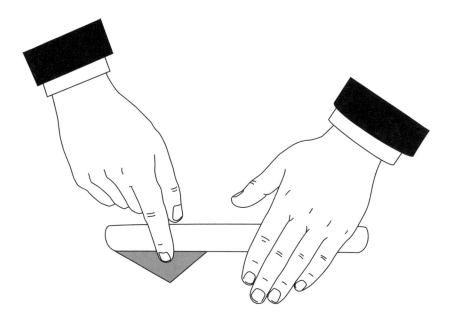

2

the upper note angled away to your right. It is important that the note on top is slightly further forward towards the audience. It does not quite meet the edges of the lower note.

2 Make sure the audience is clear which note is on top.

3 Beginning at the point of the V use your two first fingers to start rolling the notes together (illustration 1).

4 Continue rolling until only a small part of a corner of the lower note is visible on the table. When you reach this point stop rolling. More of the upper note will be sticking out as it began slightly further forward.

3

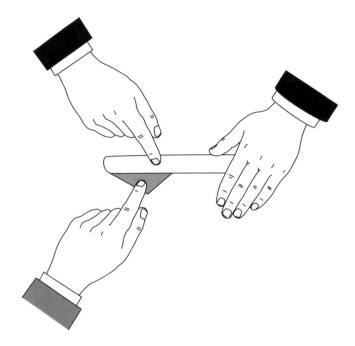

5 Cover the visible corner of the lower note with your left hand. Do this while your right finger points to the corner of the upper note sticking out on the right (illustration 2). Ask a spectator to place a finger on the corner on your right (illustration 3).

6 As they do this, secretly roll the notes forward slightly. Under cover of your left hand, the left corner will flip around the roll – it will go under the rolled up notes and flip back on to the table in its original position. This is the secret move which makes the trick work.

7 Lift your left hand and ask the spectator to place a finger from their other hand on that corner.

8 Point out to the audience that the corners of both notes are now being pinned to the table. Explain this makes any trickery impossible – unknown to them it has already happened!

9 Unroll the notes towards you and show that – incredibly – the two notes have passed through each other. The note that was on top is now below (illustration 4).

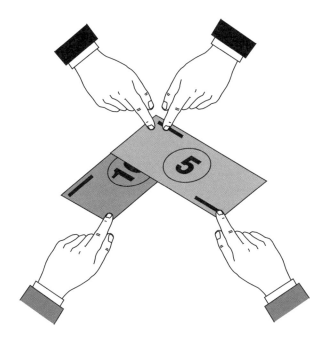

Top tips for tricksters

With a few well practised coin tricks which you can perform with any coins you will always be able to entertain friends any time, any place, anywhere!

Effect *The magician shows a piece of paper which is punched with two holes – both too small for a coin to pass through. The magician demonstrates how it is possible to make a coin pass through a hole slightly smaller than the coin, but then goes on to visibly make the coin pass through a hole less than half its size!*

Requirements *Any large coin and a piece of paper.*

Preparation *Prepare the paper with folds and cut-outs as shown in illustration 1. The large hole A should be slightly smaller than the coin you intend to use. The small hole B can be much smaller, but the cut-outs around the edges of the paper must correspond when the paper is folded.*

• •

1

3cm/1.25in   3cm/1.25in

6.25cm/2.5in

1.25cm/0.5in

A

6.25cm/2.5in

B

2.5cm/1in

1 Display the paper and coin. Hold the coin against the large hole as in illustration 2. Fold the paper in half across the diameter of the hole.

2 Bend the sides of the paper inwards (illustration 3). The hole will widen and the coin will fall through without tearing the paper.

2

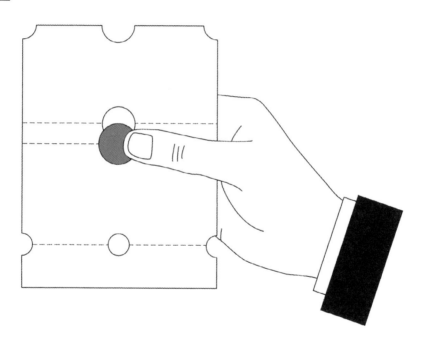

Coin tricks you can buy

CASINO COIN   This enables you to change casino chips magically into real currency.

3

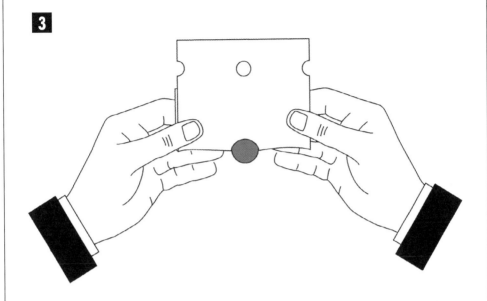

3 Now say that you will attempt the far more difficult task of making the coin pass through the smaller hole. Hold the coin in position just below the large hole (illustration 4). Fold the upper part of the paper down towards you over the coin. Fold the right and left sides away from you, making a package around the coin. Fold the bottom section up, away from you (illustration 5). It looks as if you have wrapped the coin securely, but actually the package is open at the bottom.

Top tips for tricksters

You can always learn from watching other performers – not just magicians. Watch how they treat their audience and how the audience reacts to them.

4

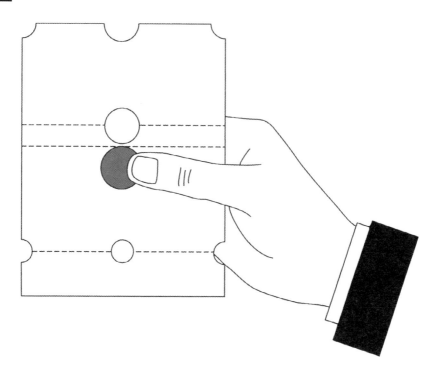

4 Keep a tight hold on the coin through the paper to prevent it slipping out prematurely through the secret opening. You are now going to complete the effect, performing it as a penetration.

Top tips for tricksters

Even though money magic is easy to do at any time it does not mean you should do it all the time. Do not hog the limelight! Wait for people to ask to see a trick.

5 Let the coin slide down to the position shown in illustration 6. Show the folded paper on all sides, apparently proving that it is impossible for the coin to escape.

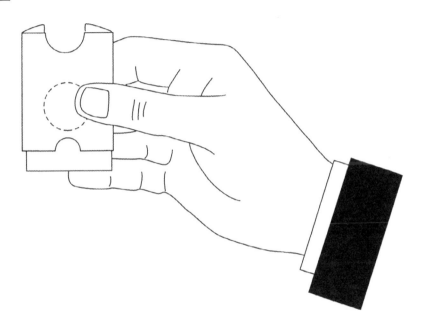

5

6 Grasp the coin (apparently through the hole) and pull it free. Unfold the paper by reversing the process described in step 3 and show that it is completely undamaged!

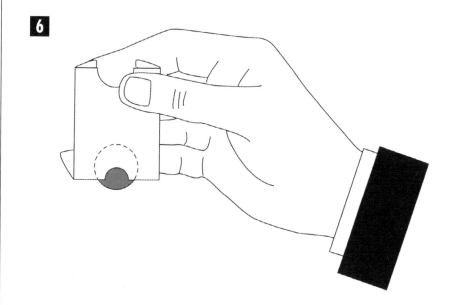

Ali Bongo

Although probably best known to the public for his work as a magic consultant for David Nixon and Paul Daniels, this Indian-born professional magician also performs in his own manic, fast-paced act as the cartoon style "Shriek of Araby". His slick presentations of the "Knife Through Balloon" and the classic "Zombie Floating Ball" are admired by the magical fraternity around the world.

Effect *A coin vanishes from inside a matchbox.*

Requirements *A small coin and a specially prepared matchbox (see "Preparation").*

Preparation *Using a razor blade or sharp knife you cut a secret flap at the bottom of one end of the matchbox drawer. Cut along the thick lines shown on illustration 2 and lightly score inside the box along the dotted line. This will create a secret flap which will open unnoticed.*

● ●

1

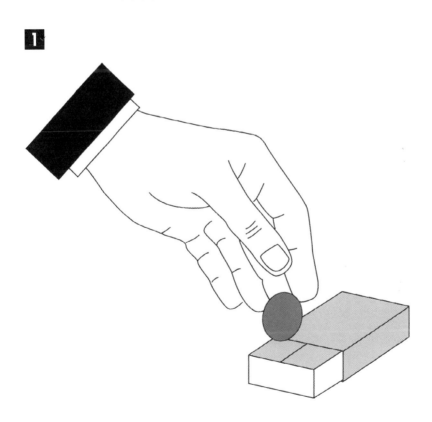

2

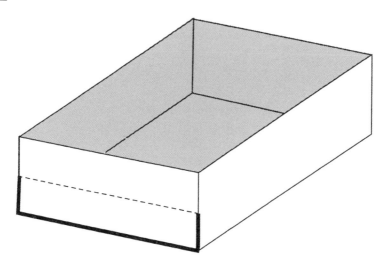

1 Push open the drawer so that the flap end remains hidden inside the cover.

2 Ask a spectator to drop the coin inside and push the drawer closed (illustration 1).

3 Pick up the box from the table and rattle it to prove the coin is inside.

Ross Bertram (1912–1992)

Ross Bertram was considered by magicians to be the true heir to the throne of T. Nelson Downs – the new "King Of Koins". He was born in Toronto, Canada. He made his first big impact upon the world of magic when he appeared at magic conventions in the USA during the 1940s.

3

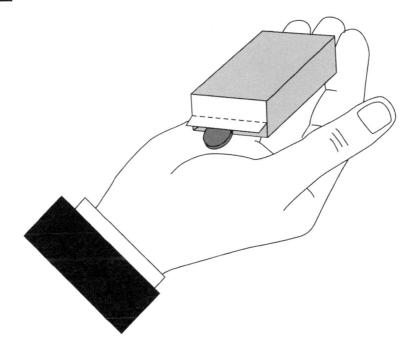

4 When you have finished rattling, allow the coin to fall through the flap into your hand where you finger palm it (illustration 3).

5 Place the (now empty) matchbox on the table and secretly pocket the coin. You can now open the matchbox to show that the coin has vanished "into thin air"!

Top tips for tricksters

Many different fake coins and coin "boxes" are available from magic shops and dealers. Some of these will be described in the following pages.

Effect *A marked coin vanishes from the magician's hand.*

Requirements *Any coin (the smaller the better), a pencil with an eraser on the end and a small piece of Blu-Tack.*

Preparation *Remove the eraser from the end of the pencil and stick the Blu-Tack inside the metal fitting that held it. Make sure plenty of Blu-Tack sticks out over the top of the fitting.*

• •

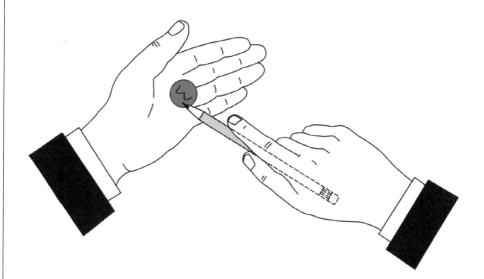

2

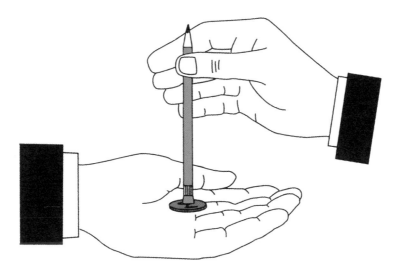

1 Hand someone the coin and the pencil and ask them to make a mark on the coin (illustration 1).

2 Take the coin and pencil back. Rest the coin mark side up on your open left hand. Hold the pencil between your right first finger and thumb. The Blu-Tack end of the pencil is hidden inside your hand.

Top tips for tricksters

Always remember that the tricks that you do are just a peg for you to hang entertainment on. If you just fool people they will be puzzled – it is the situation you create that makes it entertaining.

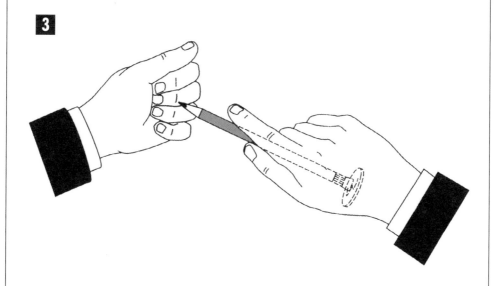

3 Bring your right hand over your left hand and tap the sticky end of the pencil on to the coin (illustration 2). Apparently you are indicating and referring to the mark made on the coin. Press hard so that the coin sticks to the end of the pencil.

4 Look at the audience to take attention away from your hands as you make some comment about the spectator's artistic ability. At this moment swing the end of the pencil – and the attached coin – into your right hand (illustration 3). At the same time close your left hand, as though it still contained the coin.

5 Tap on the back of the left hand with the pointed end of the pencil as though it were a magic wand. Place the pencil – and coin – in your pocket and open your left hand to show the coin has vanished!

Effect *A banknote vanishes inside the magician's hand.*

Requirements *A banknote.*

Preparation *The secret of this effect is the special fold which makes the banknote look like two. Prepare the note with this fold before the performance.*

Fold lines X–X and Y–Y away from you and lines A–A and B–B towards you (illustration 1). Fold the note along these creases so that it looks like illustration 2.

● ●

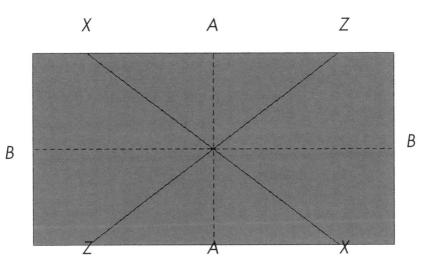

Now fold the point marked A to the right and the corresponding point B on the back to the right.

It should now look as though you have two separate banknotes (illustration 3).

• •

1 Display the folded note in your right hand, telling the audience you have two notes.

2 Show your left hand empty and place the folded note inside. Say, "The two notes go into my empty hand."

3 Close your left hand into a fist.

4 Reach into the top of your left fist with your right hand and remove the note, unfolding it as you do so. Say, "We take one away, which leaves...?"

5 After the audience have answered "one", open your hand to show that it is empty!

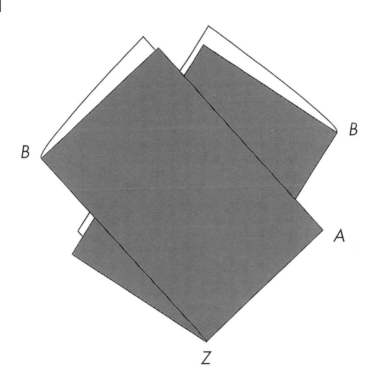

Effect *Two coins are covered with playing cards. Amazingly one coin vanishes and appears under the other card.*

Requirements *Two coins, two playing cards and a short length of thread. You will also need a good smooth surface to perform this effect.*

Preparation *Join the two coins together with the length of thread (illustration 1). The simplest way to do this is to tape an end of the thread to the bottom of each coin. The thread between the coins should be about 2.5cm/1in long. Place the prepared coins in your pocket along with your loose change.*

1

2

1 Remove a handful of change from your pocket and pick out the two prepared coins. Place them on the table (tape side down) as in illustration 1.

2 Cover the coin nearest you with a playing card (illustration 2).

3 Pick up the other playing card with your right hand, at the same time pushing the uncovered coin forward with your left hand.

4 As you do this, unknown to your audience, the covered coin will be pulled out from under the first card. This coin will be hidden by your left wrist (illustration 3).

5 The playing card in your right hand is dropped over the visible coin and covers the concealed coin at the same time.

6 Make a magical pass and then show that the coin has vanished from under the first card and both coins are now together under the second.

7 You can repeat this effect by using a different "steal" as follows. Begin with the coins side by side on the table. Cover the right coin with a card. With your left first finger push the visible coin until it is in position just next to the front short edge of the card. This "proves" to the audience that the coins are not connected.

3

8 The right hand uses the front short edge of the other card to slide the visible coin forward. Again, the second coin will be pulled along too, this time hidden below the moving card (illustration 4).

9 The right hand drops the card over both coins. Make a magical pass, and show the coin has passed again!

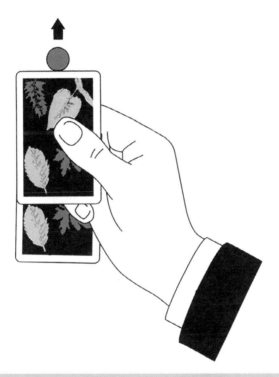

Coin tricks you can buy

CIGARETTE THROUGH COIN   As its name suggests this is a special coin through which you can push a borrowed cigarette.

Effect *This is a mighty impressive flourish to do with four coins. This is not a trick – it is just a flashy display. Be warned that this is probably the most difficult effect in the book, but if you have the patience to learn it you will be able to do a piece of coin manipulation that will prove an effective display of your skills.*

Requirements *Four identical coins.*

Preparation *None.*

● ●

1

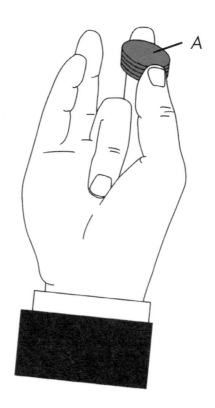

A

2

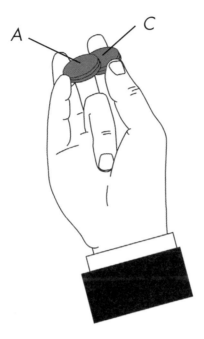

1 Stack the four coins in a pile and hold them together between your right thumb and first finger. The hand should be palm up.

2 Bend your right second finger into the palm and tilt your hand very slightly to the left (illustration 1).

3 Release the thumb's pressure on the top two coins of the stack and, using the fourth finger, rotate them until they are wedged between the third and fourth fingers (illustration 2).

4 Lift your second finger and apply pressure with it to the edges of the top coin of each pair. Your thumb and fourth finger apply pressure to the edges of the lower coin of each pair.

3

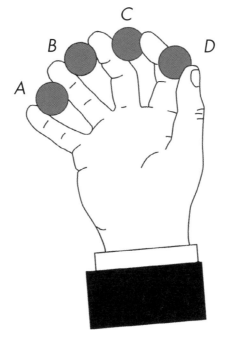

5 Slowly straighten out your fingers. Your thumb and fourth fingers pivot outwards splitting the two pairs of coins. The second finger rolls between the two centre coins holding their edges.

6 You now have a coin clipped between each finger.

Bobby Bernard

Bobby Bernard is British magic's best-known teacher, having produced many award-winning acts. He is also well known for his skill and innovative creations in the field of sleight of hand with coins. His stage act is a theatrical presentation of the magic of Isaac Fawkes, the well-known magician from the 1800s.

Effect *A coin is placed in a glass and covered with a handkerchief. At the magician's command the coin leaves the glass and appears in the centre of a ball of wool!*

Requirements *Two duplicate coins, a glass, a handkerchief, an elastic band and a ball of wool.*

Preparation *Place one of the coins in the centre of the ball of wool. Have the ball of wool near at hand.*

• •

1 Drop the coin into the glass and cover the mouth of the glass with the handkerchief. Place the elastic band over the mouth of the glass to hold the handkerchief in position. The elastic band should be around the middle of the glass, and not too tight (illustration 1).

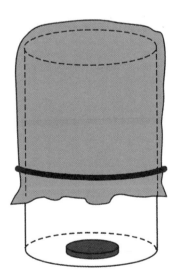

2 Pick up the glass with the left hand, sliding the handkerchief and the elastic band up about 2.5cm/1in to give you some slack in the top of the handkerchief (illustration 2).

3 Shake the glass so that the coin can be heard by the audience rattling inside. Tip the mouth of the glass towards the right hand. When you hear the coin make a clinking sound, close the right hand into a fist as though the coin had been tipped into it (illustration 3).

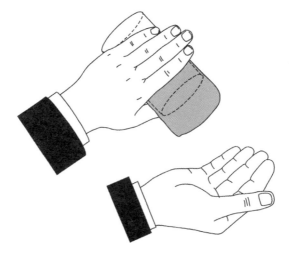

4 Replace the glass on the table. Because of the sack, the coin is now trapped in a fold of the handkerchief and is hanging outside the mouth of the glass (illustration 4). (When you place the glass on the table make sure the secret fold is hanging at the back of the glass.) The audience can see through the glass – it is empty!

5 Make a tossing motion towards the ball of wool with the right hand. Show that the right hand is empty. Show that the left hand is empty. Take hold of the fold of handkerchief with the right hand, clipping the coin through the material. Pull the handkerchief off the glass leaving the elastic band behind. Place the handkerchief in your pocket along with the coin.

6 The coin has vanished! Hand a member of the audience the ball of wool and ask them to unravel it. Inside is the coin!

4

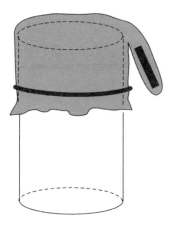

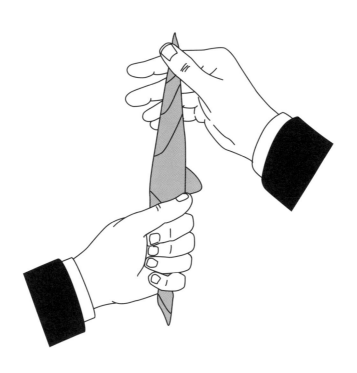

Great
Handkerchief Tricks

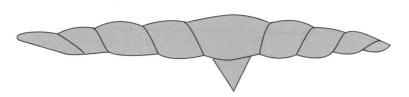

TWISTING A HANDKERCHIEF INTO A "ROPE"

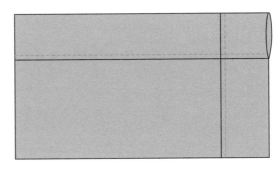

CORNER OF A HANDKERCHIEF SHOWING THE OPENING IN THE HEM

REEF KNOT

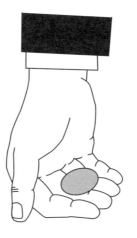

FINGER PALM OF A COIN

Effect *The magician ties a knot in the centre of a silk handkerchief. When the spectators blow on the knot it simply melts away.*

Requirements *A silk handkerchief or scarf 45 x 45cm/18 x 18in.*

Preparation *None.*

●●●●●●●●●●●●●●●●●●●●●●●

1 Hold the handkerchief by diagonally opposite corners between the first and second fingers of the left hand (end A) and the right hand (end B). Twist the handkerchief into a "rope" as shown in illustration 1.

2 Bring end B over to your left hand, passing it between your left second and third fingers, and clip end B under the left thumb (illustration 2).

1

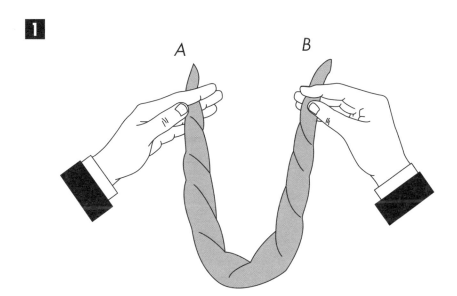

A   B

2

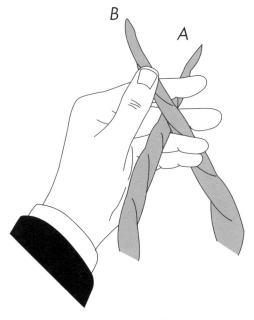

3 Your right hand now goes through the loop and takes hold of end A. Your left third and fourth fingers hold down the silk "rope" below end A (illustration 3).

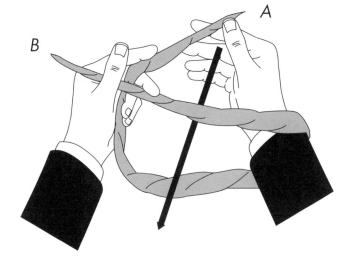

4 After the left third and fourth fingers close around the handkerchief, the left second finger clips the silk where the two ends cross (illustration 3).

5 Pull end A through the loop with your right hand. End B is held tightly between the left thumb and first finger. The left third and fourth fingers release their grip around the silk as your left second finger hooks and pulls the lower portion of end B through the loop (illustration 4).

6 As you pull on end A a knot will form around the loop held by the second finger of the left hand. Remove your left second finger from inside the loop when the knot is tight enough to hold its own shape. This appears to be a genuine knot, but it is actually a slip knot.

7 Ask the audience to blow at the knot. As they do, secretly pull on the ends. The knot will dissolve and appear to melt away.

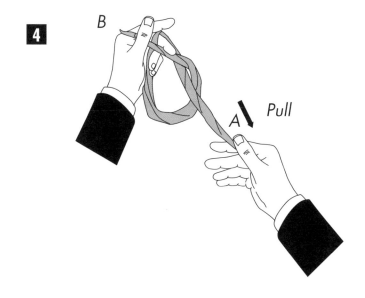

Effect *The magician makes a cone out of newspaper and pushes a silk handkerchief inside with a magic wand. The magician tears the newspaper into pieces to show that the silk handkerchief has completely vanished!*

Requirements *A newspaper, a silk handkerchief and a special magic wand (see "Preparation").*

Preparation *As the title of the effect suggests, it is the magic wand which makes the handkerchief disappear. To make this you will need a long thin hollow tube, plus a length of thin dowelling. Glue a circle of black card slightly larger than the diameter of the tube to the end of the dowelling (see illustration 1). Paint the tube black and white so that it looks like a magic wand.*

• •

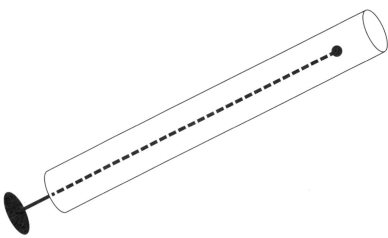

1 Form the newspaper into a cone. Rattle the magic wand inside the cone to prove it is empty. Secretly allow the rod to slide out and remain inside the cone. Drape the handkerchief over the mouth of the cone.

2 Using the magic wand you appear to push the silk down into the cone. In reality the wand slides over the rod and the rod and handkerchief are pushed up inside the hollow wand.

3 Remove the wand from the cone (with the rod and handkerchief tucked inside it) and set the wand down to one side.

4 Say the magic words and tear open the newspaper cone to show that it is completely empty!

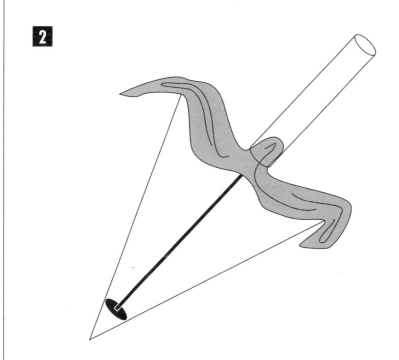

Effect *The magician places a coin under a handkerchief. One by one a number of spectators place their hands under the handkerchief to make sure the coin is still there. Despite this tight security the coin vanishes. Even though the audience can all examine the handkerchief and the magician, they cannot find the coin.*

Requirements *A handkerchief and a coin. Both can be borrowed from members of the audience.*

Preparation *You need one other vital thing, and that is a secret helper! Before your performance get a member of the audience on your side and tell them to take the coin when they feel under the handkerchief and keep it concealed in their hand!*

1

1 Borrow a handkerchief and a coin from members of the audience. Explain that the audience are going to act as your jury for this performance.

2 Roll up your sleeves so the audience cannot suspect that the coin goes up one of your sleeves.

Top tips for tricksters

To prevent your silk handkerchiefs from becoming frayed at the edges you can double hem them. Fold over the original hem and sew them again.

3 Put the coin on the palm of your hand and cover it with the handkerchief (illustration 1).

4 Invite spectators up to feel under the handkerchief to check that the coin is definitely there and that you haven't sneaked it out by sleight of hand.

5 Make sure that your secret helper is the last one to feel under the handkerchief (illustration 2). You hand them the coin which they keep concealed in their hand!

6 You can now remove the handkerchief and show that the coin has vanished.

7 Meet up with your secret helper after the show to split the profits!

It makes the effect more convincing if your secret helper behaves like a very cynical critic who really does not believe that it can be done. Then nobody will suspect that they actually did the trick for you!

Carl Hertz (1859-1924)

Carl Hertz was an American magician who toured the world with his act. In the UK he became well-known in the music halls – particularly for one trick which had everybody talking. He vanished a metal birdcage with a live bird inside from the tips of his fingers. Many suspected that the bird was harmed, and so Hertz was called to perform it at the House of Commons!

Effect *The magician hypnotizes a handkerchief and it moves mysteriously as though obeying commands.*

Requirements *A pocket handkerchief.*

Preparation *None.*

• •

1 Claim to be able to hypnotize any pocket handkerchief. This is an impressive and unusual claim and will surely gain you the interest of your audience. Explain that you need to borrow somebody's handkerchief to be "put into a trance".

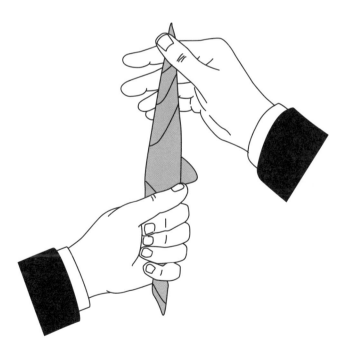

2 When you have borrowed a handkerchief spread it out flat on the table (it is always worth having a handkerchief of your own in your pocket in case nobody in your audience has one in a suitable state!).

3 Grab the top lefthand corner of the handkerchief with your left fingers and thumb, and with your right fingers and thumb hold the left edge about halfway down. Lift up the handkerchief and twist it between your hands to form a tightly twisted "rope".

4 Hold the handkerchief up vertically with your right hand at the top and the left hand below (illustration 1).

5 Keep hold with the right hand and move your left hand to a position about halfway up. As you do this make sure the handkerchief remains tightly twisted.

2

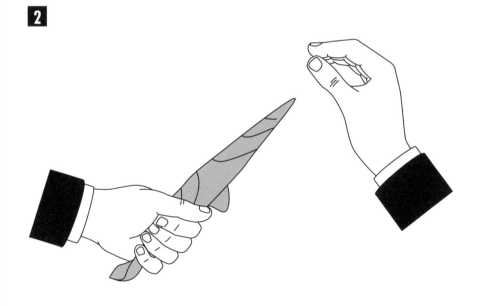

6 Pull the handkerchief tight between your hands and slowly let go with your right hand. The handkerchief will remain rigid as though hypnotized. "There you are," you say, "completely under my control!"

7 Gaze at the handkerchief and say in your most commanding tones, "Forward, forward, forward!" At the same time gently move your left thumb down the handkerchief and it will lean towards you.

8 Continue, "Back, back, back!" and move your left thumb back up the handkerchief. It will gradually slowly move away from you.

9 Repeat this a number of times, then move your left hand to hold the handkerchief horizontal to show it is rigid and completely in a trance. Say, "But it can be woken. On the count of three, when I snap my fingers it will wake up and will be unable to remember any of the things that have happened in the last few minutes!"

10 Return the handkerchief to its vertical position, click your fingers and flick open the handkerchief. Return it to its owner with a warning that it may never be the same again!

Top tips for tricksters

Magic with silk handkerchiefs is often best when performed "silently" to a musical background, without the usual magician's patter.

Effect *The magician ties a knot in the middle of a handkerchief. The handkerchief begins to move like a snake and unties the knot!*

Requirements *A silk handkerchief 45 x 45cm/18 x18in and 180cm/6ft of fine black nylon thread .*

Preparation *Attach one end of the thread to one corner of the handkerchief. Attach the other end to your table. Fold the handkerchief and place it on your table alongside the length of thread.*

• •

1 Pick up the handkerchief and stand about 1m/3ft to the side of the table. Hold the handkerchief by the corner knotted to the thread. We will call this end A. The thread should pass under your right arm to the table top. Do not worry about anybody

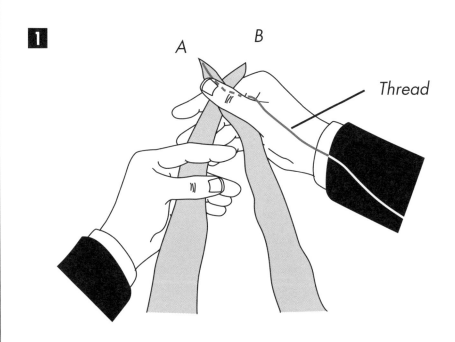

2

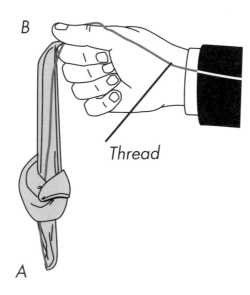

B

Thread

A

seeing the thread. The attention of the audience is on you and what you do with the handkerchief.

2 What you do with the handkerchief is to take the diagonally opposite corner to end A in your left hand (we will call this end B). Twist the handkerchief into a rope by spinning it between your hands. You should not get caught up in the thread as you do this as it passes under your arm.

3 Bring end A across and over end B and hold both ends in your right hand, adjusting your right hand so the thread passes over your right thumb (illustration 1).

4 Reach through the loop with your left hand (moving your hand towards the audience), grasp end A with the thread and pull it back through the loop.

5 Pull your hands apart slowly so that a knot forms in the centre (illustration 2). Unknown to the audience the thread passes through the loop in the knot. It is important the thread runs over your right thumb.

6 Release end A, so the handkerchief is held in the right hand. The thread is attached to the bottom corner A of the handkerchief and passes up through the knot, over your right thumb and across the table.

7 So if you move your right arm forward, the thread will pull end A up and through the knot (illustration 3). Gently move forward to pull end A up to your right hand. The knot will appear to melt away. When end A reaches your hand, release your hold of end B and grasp end A (illustration 4). Drop the handkerchief back on to your table, concluding your performance of the world's first untying knot!

3

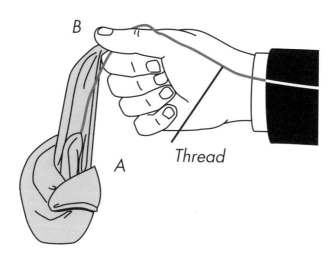

B

A

Thread

4

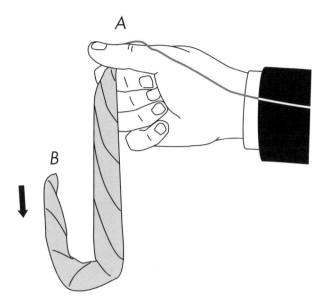

A

B

This is a stunning visual effect that is in the repertoire of many of the world's best professional magicians. It is important that you spend plenty of time practising, rehearsing and mastering this effect before you attempt to show it to anyone.

It is also possible to perform this effect without using a table. Instead of attaching the thread to the table you use a shorter length of thread, and attach one end to the handkerchief and the other end to a bead. The bead will dangle down to the floor. After you have tied the knot, put your right foot on the bead. The only other difference in the trick is that you move your right arm upwards instead of forwards to untie the knot. This method enables you to perform the effect almost impromptu.

Effect *The magician spreads his pocket handkerchief flat on the table and slowly folds the four corners to the centre. He grabs the air and claims to have captured a ghost. He places the invisible spook inside the handkerchief. Slowly a solid object forms inside the handkerchief. When the magician opens the handkerchief it is empty once again.*

Requirements *A gentleman's pocket handkerchief with a wide hem and a length of coat hanger wire.*

Preparation *Cut a length of coat hanger wire about 6.5cm/2.5in long. Carefully insert this into the hem of the handkerchief at one corner and sew it in place with a needle and thread. Keep this handkerchief in your pocket and you will always be ready to perform this baffling close-up effect.*

• •

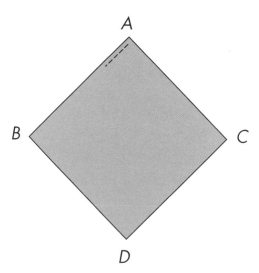

2

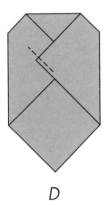

D

1 This is a great effect to do when the conversation at a party or social event has come around to ghosts, spirits and spooks. You can offer to try an experiment as you claim that they are floating around all the time.

2 Bring out the handkerchief and spread it out flat on the table with the "wire corner" A pointing towards the spectators and away from you (illustration 1).

3 Fold the wire corner A (the one furthest away from you) into the centre of the handkerchief.

4 Fold the corner B pointing to your left into the centre so that it covers the first folded corner.

5 Fold the corner C pointing to your right into the centre so that the folds on both the right and left edges are even.

Top tips for tricksters

Always have an emergency sewing kit in your "bag of tricks" when you have any hanky tricks in the act!

3

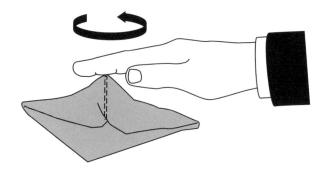

6 These three folds create a small pocket with an opening towards you (illustration 2).

7 Reach into the air with your right hand and pretend to catch one of the little ghosts floating around you. Ensure that the audience can see that your hand is really empty.

8 Your left hand lifts up the folded corners to allow you to slide your right hand into the pocket to apparently trap the ghost inside. While inside the pocket your right hand grabs the wire sewn into the hem and stands it upright on one end.

9 Remove your right hand from inside. The wire will remain standing inside and when the left hand lets go of the corners it

Top tips for tricksters

Tricks with silk handkerchiefs are not particularly suitable for outdoor shows like garden parties and fêtes as they can easily be ruined by a gust of wind!

will appear that "something" has solidified inside the handkerchief. This is a very spooky illusion.

10 To prove further that it is a solid object, stretch your right hand out flat and rest it on top of the handkerchief so that the end of the wire presses against your fingers. While pressing down slightly move your hand in a small circular motion, creating the illusion of a solid round object (illustration 3).

11 Borrow a spoon from the dinner table and hit the top of the secret wire with the back of the bowl of the spoon. The sound of metal on metal is very convincing and the object sounds solid (illustration 4).

12 Return the spoon and flick open the handkerchief in an attempt to see the ghost. But the ghost is too quick for you – and you are left with two empty hands, an empty handkerchief and a freaked-out bunch of friends!

4

This is based on the "Dissolving Knot" and it is highly recommended that you learn and perfect that effect before attempting this one.

Effect *The magician displays two silk handkerchiefs, which are then twisted into ropes. A spectator holds one outstretched between his hands. The handkerchiefs are securely knotted around each other, creating two knotted linked loops of silk. Like the classic "Chinese Linking Rings" the handkerchiefs seem to melt apart with their knots still intact.*

A   B

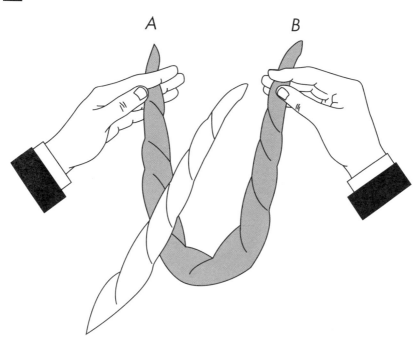

Requirements *Two silk handkerchiefs 45 x 45cm/18 x 18in, preferably of contrasting colours.*

Preparation *None.*

• •

1 Hold the first handkerchief by its diagonally opposite corners and twist it into a rope. Hand it to a member of the audience, requesting them to hold on tightly to the two ends.

2 Twist the second handkerchief and thread it underneath the first (illustration 1). Hold an end of your handkerchief in each hand.

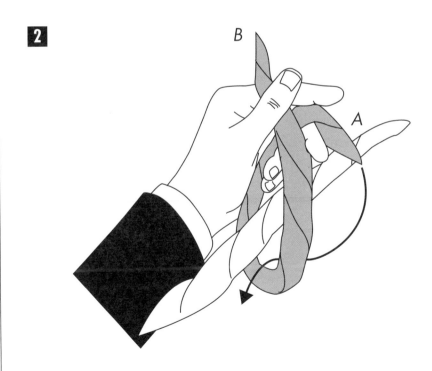

3

3 Move the right-hand end (end B) over to the left hand and clip the two ends exactly as in the "Dissolving Knot" (illustration 2). Insert your right hand through the loop and grab end A. Pull this end back through the loop to form the "Dissolving Knot".

4 Pull the two ends of your rope in opposite directions to tighten the knot. As you do this, keep your left second finger in the small loop. When the knot becomes tight you can slide out your left finger and the knot will hold itself together.

5 Loop your handkerchief underneath the spectator's handkerchief again and tie a regular secure reef knot (see Glossary, page 132) above the slip knot to make "an unbreakable circle of silk" (illustration 3).

6 Ask the spectator to tie the two ends of his handkerchief together in a secure knot. As they do this, hold on to the slip knot to ensure it is not accidentally pulled apart. It seems that the two handkerchiefs are now securely linked together.

7 Ask the spectator to hold on to the two ends of their handkerchief. You do the same with yours. Get the audience to blow on the handkerchiefs as you gently pull. The slip knot will dissolve and the two handkerchiefs will melt apart in a very magical fashion.

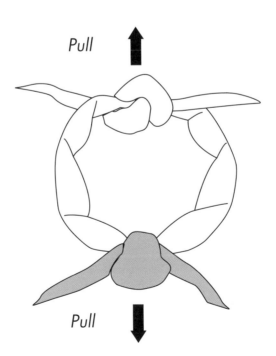

4

Pull

Pull

Effect *A silk handkerchief – representing the world-famous escape artiste Harry Houdini – escapes from a sealed glass tumbler.*

Requirements *Two different coloured silk handkerchiefs, a large silk scarf, 25cm/10in of cotton thread, a glass tumbler and an elastic band.*

Preparation *Tie the cotton thread to one corner of the handkerchief that you want to "escape".*

• •

1 Tell the audience about the exploits of the Great Houdini and his ability to escape from any confinement – prison cell, packing case, straitjacket or handcuffs. Explain that your audience are very fortunate because for the first time ever you are going to introduce the reincarnation of Houdini – as a silk handkerchief!

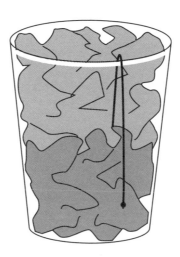

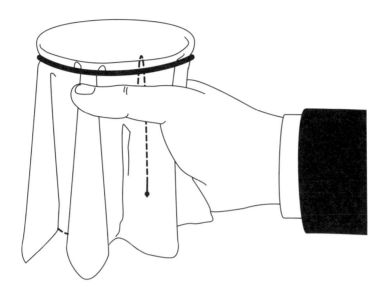

2 Display the "Houdini silk" to the audience and push it down into the bottom of the empty tumbler. As you do this make sure that you leave the thread hanging outside the glass.

3 Introduce the second handkerchief as a prison guard and stuff it into the tumbler on top of the first handkerchief (illustration 1).

4 To make extra sure that the handkerchief is unable to escape, throw the scarf over the mouth of the tumbler and hold it in place with the elastic band (illustration 2). You could call this the padded cell – or perhaps this is taking the analogy a bit too far!

5 Now tell the audience that this escape used to take 30 minutes! But today you intend to double that time! After a suitable build-up of tension, reach up under the scarf and take hold of the thread (this will be a lot easier if you tied a knot in the end of the thread).

6 Pull the thread, and the Houdini silk will be pulled out of the glass. You need to experiment to make sure that you are using an elastic band that is loose enough to enable you to do this.

7 Once the corner of the handkerchief has been pulled past the rubber band, grab hold of it and pull it sharply downwards, making it look as if the silk has penetrated through the bottom of the glass. Houdini lives on to escape once again!

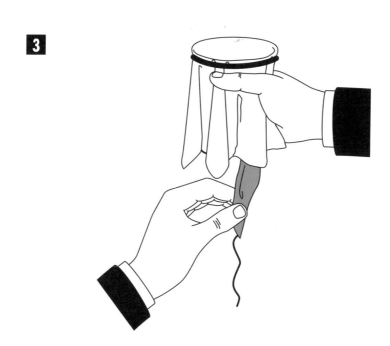

3

This apparently extraordinary and impossible penetration effect works on the fiendishly simple principle of secretly turning the glass upside down under the cover of the handkerchief.

Effect *A handkerchief is placed inside a drinking glass. It is then trapped inside it by placing a second handkerchief over the mouth of the glass, and securing it with a tight rubber band. Even though a member of the audience holds on to the glass, the handkerchief still manages to escape!*

Requirements *Two cotton handkerchiefs, a rubber band and a straight-sided drinking glass (that is, the diameter of the base and the mouth should be the same).*

Preparation *None.*

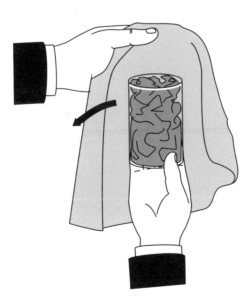

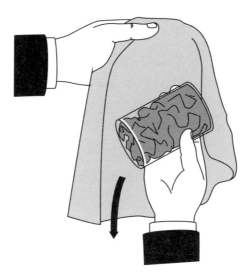

1 Ask a member of the audience to examine the glass to ensure there are no trap doors, secret passages or hidden keys to enable the handkerchief to escape! Meanwhile the handkerchief that is to escape can be subjected to an extensive "body search".

2 When the props have been examined, take them back and hold the empty drinking glass with the tips of the fingers and thumb of your right hand. Ask a member of the audience to put the handkerchief in the glass, and push it down to the bottom. It is important that you use a large handkerchief, so that when the glass is turned upside down it will not fall out, but cling to the glass.

3 To make an "air-tight container" you apparently drape the second handkerchief over the mouth of the glass and seal it with

3

the elastic band. But in fact it is here that you perform the secret move! Bring the handkerchief up in front of the glass to cover it from the audience's view for just a moment. At this moment your right hand relaxes its grip on the bottom of the glass and pivots it between your thumb and fingers, turning the glass upside down.

4 The left hand drapes its handkerchief over the now reversed glass and the right hand. Grip the glass with the left hand through the handkerchief and remove the right hand from under the handkerchief. Pick up the elastic band and apparently seal the top of the glass. In reality you are sealing the bottom!

5 Ask a member of the audience to come up and hold on to the sides of the glass. Ensure they do not put their fingers too near the elastic band, or they may feel that the "top" has sealed over with glass and realize it is really the bottom of the glass!

6 Show that both your hands are empty, roll up your sleeves and then dramatically reach under the covering handkerchief and pull out the handkerchief from inside the glass (illustration 3). Apparently it has penetrated right through the bottom of the glass.

7 After the applause has died down, take back the glass from the spectator. Reach underneath with the right hand and rest the edge of the mouth of the glass on the tips of the right thumb and fingers. With the left hand pull up the handkerchief so that the elastic band slides up too. When the elastic band has been released, pause while you pivot the glass in your right hand back to its starting position (illustration 4).

8 When the glass is back in its original position, take away the covering handkerchief. Show the empty undamaged glass and hand everything out for examination. Sit back and await more applause!

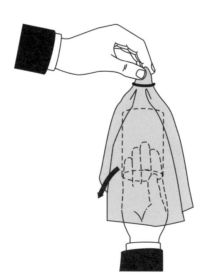

Effect *This is a startling opening effect. The magician shows both hands empty. After making a grab in the air a silk handkerchief appears in the magician's hands!*

Requirements *A silk handkerchief about 45 x 45cm/18 x 18in.*

Preparation *Spread the handkerchief out flat on a table. Fold the four corners into the middle so that they almost touch (illustrations 1 and 2). Repeat, folding the four new corners into the centre. Continue folding until you have a bundle about 5cm/2in across.*

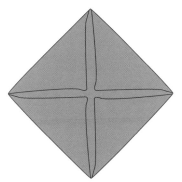

3

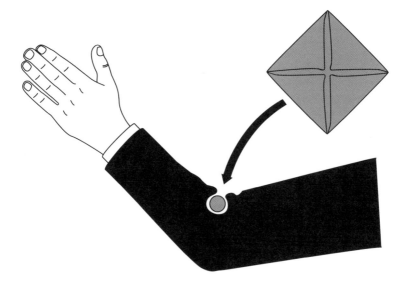

Place the folded handkerchief in the bend of your elbow (illustration 3) just before you begin your performance. If you keep your arm bent, the handkerchief will remain concealed.

● ●

This effect is over in just a few seconds, but it appears to be quite magical.

1 Show the audience that both your hands are empty by wiggling your fingers.

2 Look upwards. Quickly reach up with both hands and, as you do this, straighten your arms. The handkerchief will be propelled into the air (illustration 4).

3 Catch the handkerchief between your hands. It seems to have appeared in mid air.

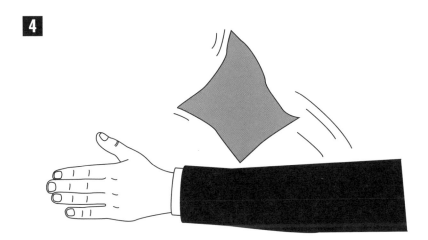

4

Robert Houdin (1805–1871)

Robert Houdin was a French watchmaker who became a magician and the talk of Paris with his Soirées Fantastiques at his own specially-built theatre. He revolutionized magic and is credited as being "The Father of Modern Magic". He used his mechanical skills to build many of his effects. In one of the most famous, a lady's handkerchief was borrowed and vanished. Flowers and fruit appeared on a nearby orange tree. One of the oranges opened and two butterflies flew out carrying the borrowed handkerchief, which was then returned to its astonished owner.

Effect *After showing that two tubes are both completely empty, the magician produces silk handkerchiefs and ribbons from within.*

Requirements *Two tubes about 30cm/12in high and 15cm/6in diameter, which fit one inside the other (it may be easiest to make the tubes to size using stiff paper held together with paper clips), a paper clip, about 15cm/6in of dark thread, elastic bands and your production "load" – ribbons and silk handkerchiefs.*

1

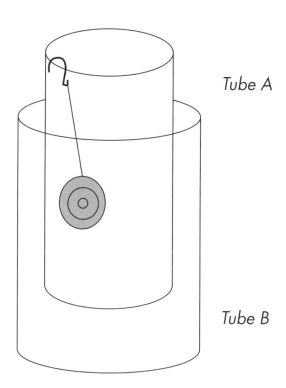

Tube A

Tube B

Preparation *Roll up the handkerchiefs and ribbons into a compact bundle and hold it together with the elastic bands. Bend the paper clip into an S-shaped hook. Attach one end of the thread to the hook and the other end to one of the elastic bands. Hook the clip over the top edge of the thinner tube (tube A) with the bundle dangling inside out of sight. We will call the wider of the two tubes tube B. Set tubes A and B next to each other on the table.*

• •

2

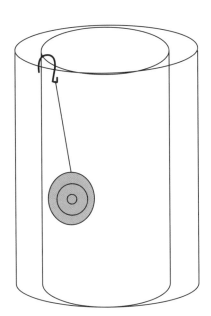

1 Pick up both tubes, one in each hand. Hold up tube B so that the audience can see through it and see that it is empty.

2 Slide tube A into the top of tube B, making sure that the hook clips on to the top of tube B (illustration 2).

3 Allow tube A to slide out of the bottom of tube B. The bundle should remain hanging out of sight inside tube B. You can now hold up tube A to show the audience that it is completely empty.

4 Slide tube A back into tube B from the bottom, so that the bundle is now hanging inside both tubes (illustration 3). Roll up your sleeves and show the audience that your hands are completely empty. Reach inside the tubes and remove the elastic

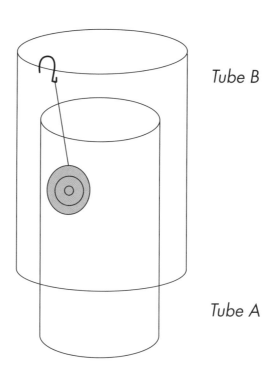

3

Tube B

Tube A

bands from around the bundle. Dramatically remove the ribbons and handkerchiefs from inside the nested tubes (illustration 4).

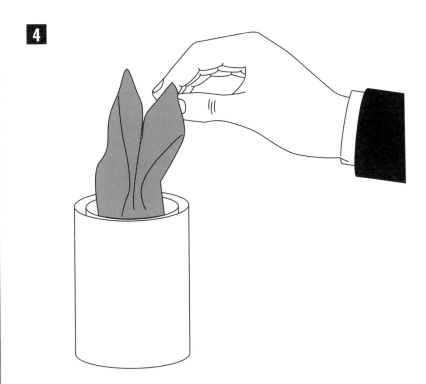

4

Effect *This is a great opening effect. The magician shows both sides of a handkerchief. He then drapes it over his hand and a form appears underneath – it is a full glass of wine!*

Requirements *An opaque handkerchief about 60 x 60cm/ 24 x 24in square, a piece of cloth to match the jacket you will wear when you perform, a full wine glass and cover (see below).*

Preparation *Put the wine glass on the cloth that matches your jacket and draw around the base. Cut out the circle and stick it securely on the base. Make sure the liquid is sealed inside the glass with a cover. You can make this with a piece of clingfilm held over the mouth of the glass with an elastic band (illustration 1).*

Fill the glass and seal it. Position the glass with the base at the front under your left armpit – the stem of the glass runs under

your armpit. Because of the extra piece of material on the base of the glass it is camouflaged against your jacket. Now you see why this has to be your opening effect! Drape the handkerchief over your left arm and you are ready to amaze your audience.

• •

1 Both hands hold the handkerchief at the corners of the top edge. The thumbs grip over the hem with the fingers concealed behind the handkerchief (illustration 2).

2 Turn the handkerchief around to show there is nothing on the other side. You do this by crossing your arms. Your right hand moves behind your left arm. Your left hand moves to the right to stop in front of your right elbow (illustration 3).

3 In this position your right fingers clip the stem of the wineglass. When the fingers are gripping the base, relax your pressure with your left arm and the glass will swing upside down out of sight behind the handkerchief. This all happens as you are apparently just displaying the handkerchief.

4 Move your hands back to their original positions. The upside down glass is kept concealed behind the handkerchief, with the right fingers clipping the stem (illustration 4).

3

4

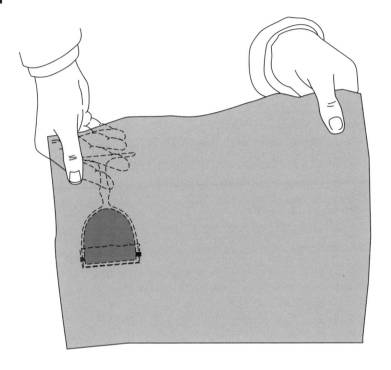

5 The right thumb releases its hold on the corner of the handkerchief and the right hand, with the glass clipped between its fingers, slides under the handkerchief to the approximate centre. It seems that the handkerchief covers your empty right hand. The glass is concealed in the drapes of the handkerchief.

6 The left hand lets go of its corner and pulls straight up on the centre of the handkerchief. As you do this be careful you do not pull too far otherwise the glass will be revealed hanging from the right hand.

7 The right fingers curl into the palm of your hand bringing the glass up with them. The left hand releases its hold on the centre of the handkerchief and it falls over the glass. To the audience it seems impossible for anything to have appeared under the handkerchief.

8 The left fingers take hold of the centre of the handkerchief and, through the fabric, remove the cover on the mouth of the glass as they pull up the handkerchief to reveal a full glass of wine (illustration 5). The cover is taken away in the handkerchief and both are discarded to one side. Give the drink to a member of your audience to confirm it is real, and joke that "all my tricks look better when you've had a drink!"

Effect *The magician displays a sealed prediction. A number of different coloured squares are dropped into the middle of a handkerchief and a member of the audience reaches in and removes one square. The prediction reveals that the magician knew which colour would be chosen. Spooky!*

Requirements *Two identical patterned pocket handkerchiefs, several small squares of card (about 2.5cm/1in square) all different colours (red, yellow, blue, green, orange, brown, black and white) and several squares of card all the same colour (red) and a prediction reading, "You will choose red."*

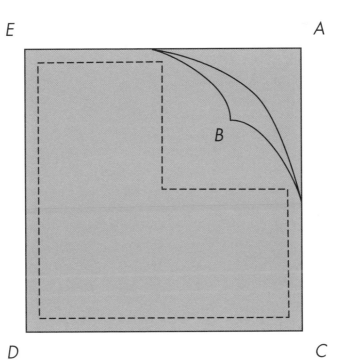

E   A

B

D   C

Preparation *You have to ensure that your volunteer chooses a red card by "forcing" it on them. To do this, you need to make a special handkerchief with a secret pocket. Place the two handkerchiefs one on top of the other and sew them together as shown in illustration 1 to make a secret pocket in one corner. In this secret pocket you put all the identical coloured (red) squares. You need to set up the handkerchief so that you can leave it on your table, and pick it up without any of the hidden squares spilling out.*

• •

1 Hand your sealed prediction to a member of the audience, who will be the "guardian of the envelope".

2 Hold the handkerchief in one hand by the secret pocket corner. Fold up the other three corners to make a bag. After showing all the coloured squares to be different, drop them into the centre of the handkerchief (illustration 2). Make sure they do not go into the secret pocket or you'll be in real trouble!

3 Shake up the handkerchief to mix the squares and ask a spectator to dip into the handkerchief and take out one square – this will be their freely chosen colour. When you offer the handkerchief to the spectator you actually open up one side of the secret pocket, so that they reach into the compartment full of red squares. Unknown to them, it doesn't matter which square they pull out – it's going to be red!

4 After the spectator has shown everyone their selected red square, dump the handkerchief to one side. Do not open the handkerchief again, as someone may see that the one red square is still among the selection of different colours! And be particularly careful not to let all the red squares fall out, or you will look very stupid!

5 Ask the "guardian of the envelope" to open it and read out your prediction. Once again the wonder magician has successfully predicted the future!

You can use the fake handkerchief to perform quite a few similar effects.

2

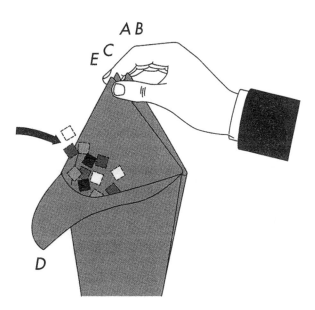

Effect *After the wave of a magic wand the magician produces a silk handkerchief from his hands, which were empty moments before. Another wave of the wand and the handkerchief changes colour!*

Requirements *A magic wand and two contrasting silk handkerchiefs – say, red and yellow.*

Preparation *Fold the four corners of each handkerchief to the centre. Then roll each one into a tube and wrap them alongside each other around one end of the wand (illustration 1). To perform this as an opener, hold the wand in your right hand, with your hand concealing the handkerchiefs. To perform later, set the wand on your table with other props covering the handkerchiefs.*

● ●

1

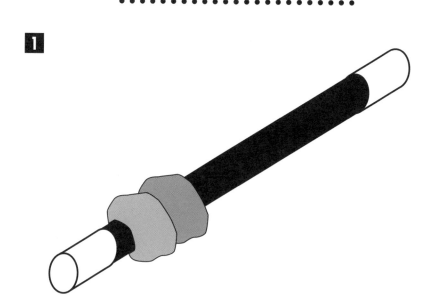

2

3

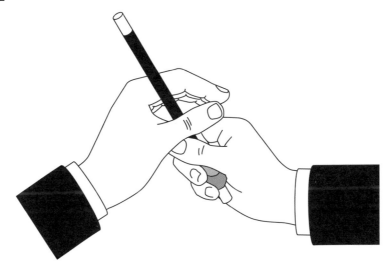

1 Begin with the wand in the right hand (illustration 2). Tap the empty left hand with the free end of the wand as you say, "My left hand is empty . . ."

2 Slide the left hand up the wand until the two hands meet (illustration 3). The left hand grasps the end of the wand, covering the two handkerchiefs. The wand pivots to the right and the right hand is shown to be empty as you say, ". . . and the right too".

3 The left hand keeps hold of the lower of the two handkerchiefs, as the right hand takes the wand back concealing the other handkerchief on the wand. We will assume the handkerchief in the left hand is red and the one still on the wand is yellow.

4

5

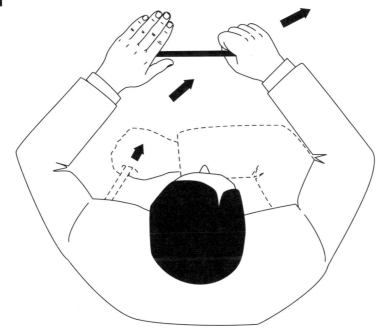

4 The right hand places the wand under the left arm so that the handkerchief is concealed under the left armpit and the free end sticks out in front (illustration 4).

5 The right hand points to the left hand, which reaches forward and snaps out the red silk handkerchief – apparently from nowhere!

6 When the applause from this production has died down, continue by rolling up the red handkerchief into a ball. This goes into your left hand while you make a magical pass with your right hand. Open your left hand to show that nothing has happened.

7 Roll the handkerchief up again, but this time keep it concealed in your right hand while pretending it is in your closed left fist.

8 The right hand (holding the red handkerchief concealed) reaches for the free end of the wand and moves it down (illustration 5) behind your left arm (which acts as a screen) and into the left hand which opens briefly to secretly "steal" the yellow handkerchief from the end of the wand. The wand continues moving.

9 Wave the wand over the closed left fist and open it to show that the handkerchief has now changed colour.

When performed correctly this is a very baffling and convincing effect, but it is highly recommended that you rehearse it many times in front of a mirror to ensure that your timing is correct and that in step 8 the yellow handkerchief remains concealed from the audience.

Houdin and Houdini

In 1856 Robert Houdin was sent by the French government to Algiers to quell the revolution by proving that French magic was stronger than African magic! On his return he wrote of his adventures in The Memoirs of Robert Houdin. *Nearly 30 years later a young Hungarian boy in America read the book and decided to become a magician. He based his stage name on that of his hero – and became Houdini!*

Effect *A match is wrapped in the folds of a handkerchief and a member of the audience snaps it into several pieces. The magician unfolds the handkerchief to show the match is restored and is completely undamaged.*

Requirements *A pocket handkerchief with a wide hem and a box of matches.*

Preparation *Take one of the matches and slide it into the open end of the hem (illustration 1). Push it inside until it is concealed from view.*

• •

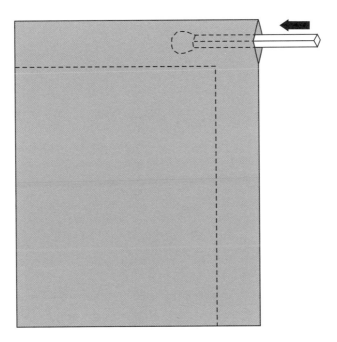

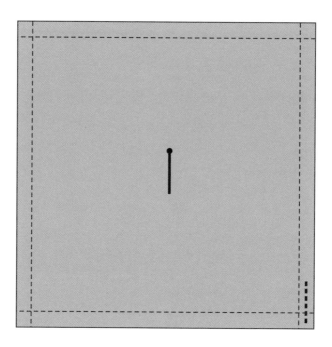

1 Bring out the box of matches and open them. Ask a member of the audience to "pick a match, any match!" and take it out of the box.

2 Bring out the handkerchief and spread it out flat on the table. Ensure that the corner with the match in it is nearest you.

3 Ask the spectator to place their freely selected match in the middle of the handkerchief (illustration 2).

4 Fold the "hidden match corner" over the selected match (illustration 3). Next fold the diagonally opposite corner over on top, followed by the last two corners.

5 Now feel through the folds of the handkerchief for the secret match. The selected match will remain hidden inside the folds of the handkerchief.

6 Hand the match, wrapped in the folds of the handkerchief, to the spectator and tell them to break the match several times (illustration 4). They believe they are breaking their selected match, but in fact they break the secret match which is hidden in the hem.

7 When the spectator is convinced the match has been completely destroyed, slowly and dramatically unfold the corners of the handkerchief. The audience will be amazed to see that the broken match has now been completely restored.

Hand the match out for examination, and take the opportunity to stuff the handkerchief in your pocket!

3

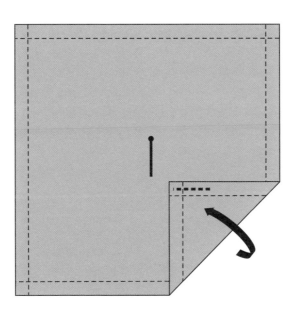

4

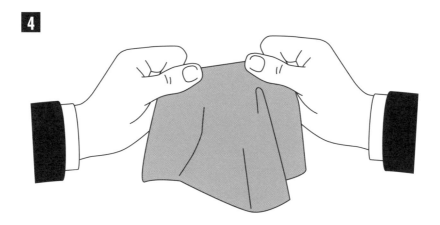

Maskelyne (1839–1917) and Devant (1868–1941)

In the early 1900s John Nevil Maskelyne and David Devant were England's most famous magicians running "England's Home of Mystery" firstly at the Egyptian Hall and later at St George's Hall in London. Devant was a charming gentleman on stage (his publicity proclaimed, "All Done By Kindness"), while Maskelyne was an acclaimed inventor and creator. Among Maskelyne's inventions was Psycho, a card-playing, mind-reading automaton. Together the two magicians were an unbeatable team and their sell-out shows were a "must" on any trip to London at the turn of the century.

Effect *Two silk handkerchiefs are tied together and put on one side. A third silk handkerchief vanishes and re-appears in an impossible place – tied between the other two!*

Requirements *Four silk handkerchiefs – two of a matching plain colour (red) and two matching multi-coloured ones. It is important that a corner of the multi-coloured handkerchiefs matches the plain red ones.*

Preparation *Prepare one of the plain red handkerchiefs by folding it in half diagonally and sewing the two halves together about 4cm/1.5in away from the folded edge (illustration 1). Use sewing thread the same colour as the silk so that the secret preparation will not be visible to the audience. Tie corner D of the prepared red silk to the corner of the multi-coloured silk that is diagonally opposite its matching red corner (illustration 1). Starting at the tied end, push the multi-coloured silk into the secret pocket in the prepared handkerchief until only the red corner sticks out (illustration 2). It should appear that this is the corner of the red handkerchief.*

• •

1 Display the two red handkerchiefs and apparently tie them together. In fact you tie the corner of the genuine red handkerchief to the corner of the multi-coloured silk hidden in the secret pocket. Now place the tied handkerchiefs somewhere on view. You can place them inside an empty tumbler or glass – or invite a member of the audience to hold the handkerchiefs balled up between their hands. That way there is no way you can get at them.

1

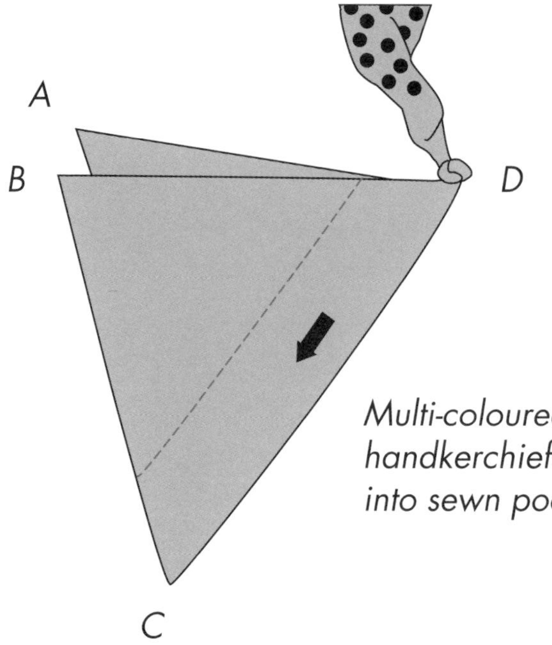

A

B

D

Multi-coloured silk handkerchief is pushed into sewn pocket

C

2

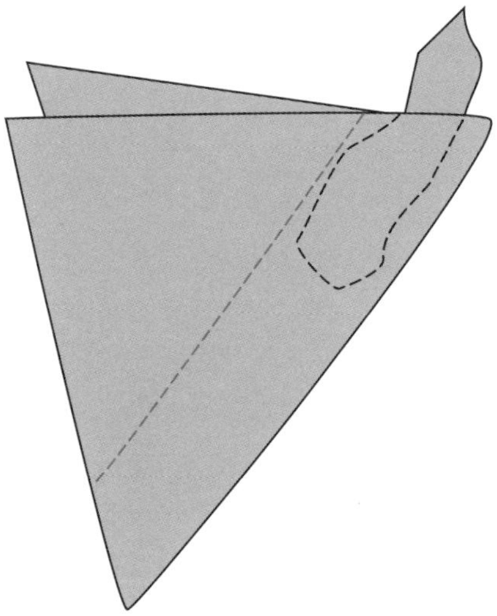

2 Vanish the duplicate multi-coloured silk handkerchief. You could use the "Paper Bag Vanish" or "Vanish in Newspaper".

3 Grab one corner of the two tied handkerchiefs and pull them out sharply. This pulls the hidden multi-coloured handkerchief from the secret pocket, and the audience see the handkerchief which apparently vanished just seconds before is now tied between the two red silk handkerchiefs (illustration 3).

If you invited a member of the audience up to hold on to the tied handkerchiefs you could say that they will never be trusted by their friends again!

3

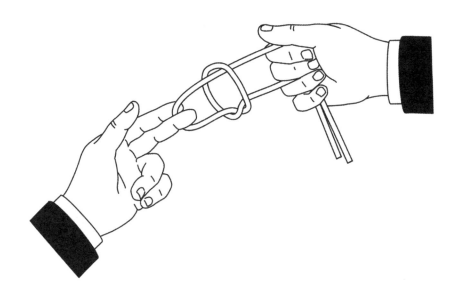

Great Rope
and
Ring Tricks

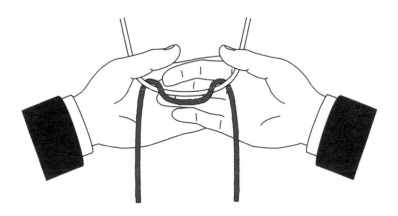

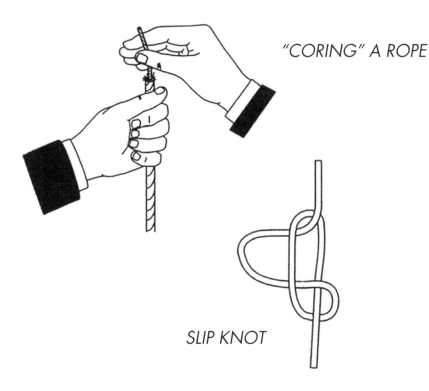

"CORING" A ROPE

SLIP KNOT

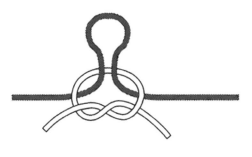

"POP OFF" KNOT

OVERHAND KNOT

Effect *The magician ties a knot in a rope using only one hand.*

Requirements *A piece of rope about 65cm/25in long.*

Preparation *There is no preparation for this version of the trick – you really do tie a knot with one hand.*

• •

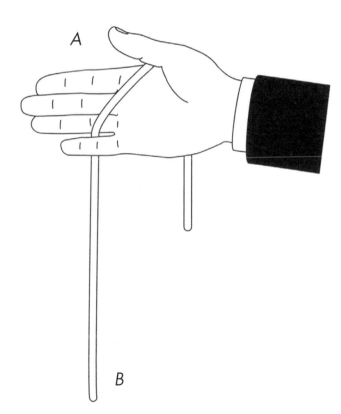

A

B

2

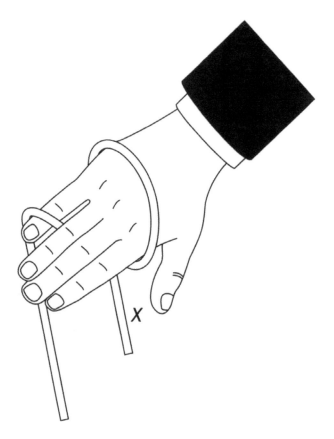

X

1 Drape the rope over your right hand as shown in illustration 1. The end hanging at the back should be slightly shorter than the end hanging at the front.

Rope preparation tip

To make your rope even more flexible you can remove the inner core. This is known as "coring" a rope.

2 Clip the rope between the little and third fingers of the right hand, as shown in illustration 1.

3 Turn your right hand over so that your thumb points to the floor, as shown in illustration 2.

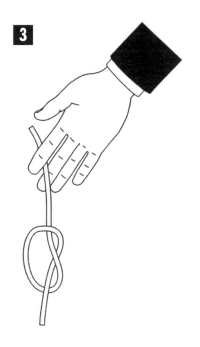

4 As your hand twists, your first and second fingers bend inwards and catch hold of the rope at the back just below the hand (at X on illustration 2). Give the rope a shake so that it falls off your hand. The piece of rope held by the first and second fingers will be pulled through the loop to form a knot (illustration 3).

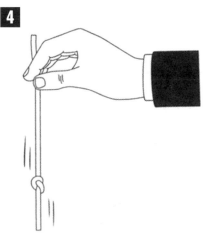

5 As the rope falls, grab the other end with your left hand and pull it tight.

6 A knot will appear in the middle of the rope – as if by magic (illustration 4).

Effect *A knot mysteriously appears in the centre of a length of rope.*

Requirements *A rope about 75cm/30in long.*

Preparation *No preparation is required.*

• •

1 Hold end A of the rope in the left hand with the end pointing up. Drape end B over the back of the right hand so that end B rests in the right palm (illustration 1).

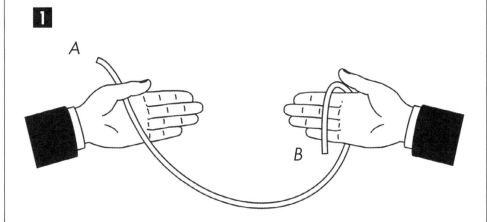

Top tips for tricksters

When using newspaper for your tricks, remember to rub over the newsprint with a tissue to remove any excess ink. This will ensure that you finish your performance as clean as you started!

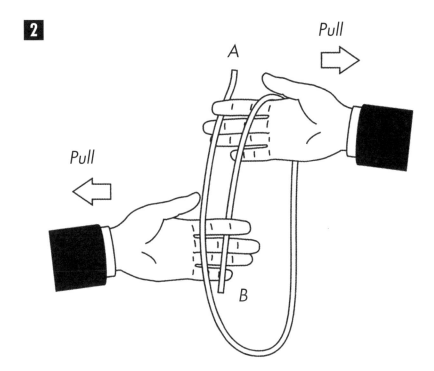

2 Move your hands towards each other. The right-hand first and second fingers clip end A above the left hand. At the same time the left-hand first and second fingers clip end B (illustration 2). As your hands move together ask a spectator to time you with their watch to see how long it takes you to tie a knot in the centre of the rope. You can explain that it takes most people about ten seconds.

Rope preparation tip

To "core" a length of rope, open the threads at one end, grasp the inner core and slide off the outer shell by pulling on the core and bunching up the shell.

3 Pull the hands apart and a knot will appear in the centre of the rope (illustration 3). Done quickly, this looks really magical. Ask your "timekeeper" how long that took you. They probably won't even have started timing you – which creates a very amusing situation.

3

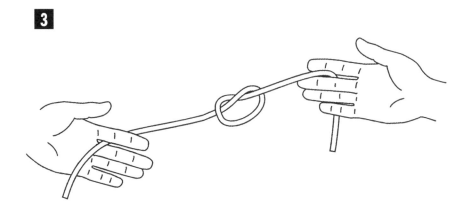

Harry Houdini (1874–1926)

Houdini was famed all over the world for his daring and dangerous escapes from packing cases, handcuffs, straitjackets – and rope. Although some of the escapes described in this book may seem simple, a number of the methods were used by Houdini to help make him into the legend he is today. He died after a student punched him in the stomach to see if he was as powerful as he claimed. This was on the 31 October 1926 (Halloween). For ten years, his wife tried to contact his spirit on this date, but failed every time. She gave up, saying, "Ten years is enough to wait for any man."

Effect *The magician ties two ropes together with a knot. When the ends are pulled the knot jumps off leaving the magician with one rope.*

Requirements *A short piece of rope about 15cm/6in long, and a longer piece about 1m/3ft.*

Preparation *Loop the two ropes and hold them together in the left hand so that they appear to be two separate ropes of the same length (illustration 1).*

1

Short piece

Long piece

This shows that the ropes are not looped together. You can hold them in place by putting your thumb over the join.

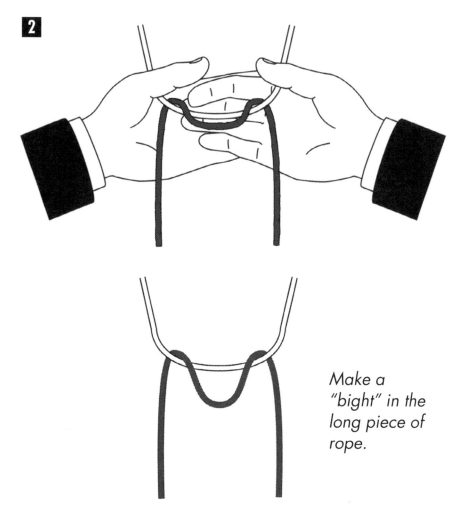

2

Make a "bight" in the long piece of rope.

1 Display the rope as two pieces of rope of equal length (illustration 1). Explain that neither rope is long enough so you are going to tie them together.

2 The right first finger pushes the centre of the long piece through the loop of the short piece (illustration 2). This forms a loop or "bight" in the long rope.

3 Now tie an overhand knot in the short piece of rope around the bight. It appears that you have tied the two ropes together. Say that the knot looks untidy, but you can fix this by asking everyone in the audience to shout "jump" on the count of three.

4 Count up to three, and when the audience shouts "jump" pull on the ends of the long piece of rope. The knot will jump off (illustration 3) and the long piece of rope will be the perfect length for your next trick!

As you can see, this is a good opening trick for a short routine of ring and rope tricks.

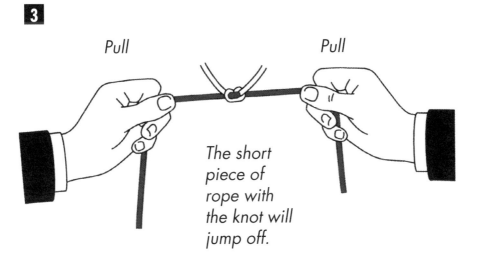

3

Pull   Pull

The short piece of rope with the knot will jump off.

Rope preparation tip

You can sew the ends of the rope to "fix" them and prevent them fraying, or simply wrap the ends in white cotton to stop them unravelling.

Effect *A knot dissolves when it is pulled.*

Requirements *A length of rope at least 60cm/2ft.*

● ●

1

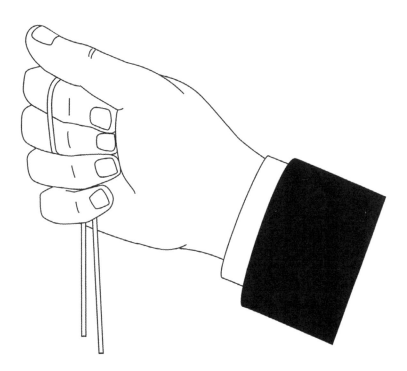

Rope preparation tip

It is a good idea to "fix" the ends of any pieces of rope you may be using in your performance as this will prevent them from fraying.

2

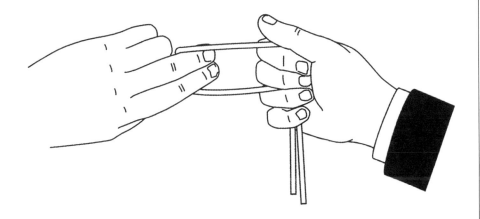

1 Make a loop at the centre of the rope and hold this in the right hand with one strand going between the thumb and first finger and the other between the second and third finger (illustration 1).

2 With the first and second fingers of the left hand pull the loop out to the left about 8cm/3in (illustration 2).

Rope preparation tip

One way to "fix" the ends of a length of rope to stop them fraying is to dip them in white glue (for example, Copydex) and allow them to dry overnight.

3

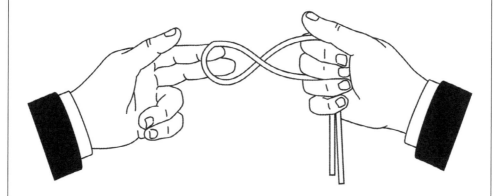

3 Twist the left hand to put a single twist in the loop (illustration 3).

4

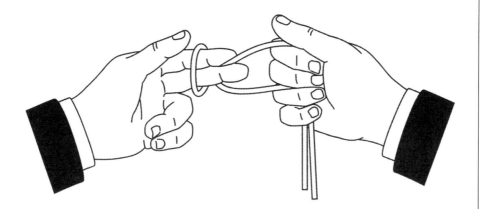

4 Slide the left first and second fingers through the loop and clip hold of the upper strand of rope (illustration 4). Pull the clipped strand through the loop to the left, and allow the loop to slip off the left fingers (illustration 5).

5 This will form a noose. Pull the ends to tighten the loop so that it looks like a knot (illustration 6).

This special knot can be used in many different tricks. The technique described teaches you how to prepare the knot secretly. With practice you will be able to tie this knot in front of an audience without arousing suspicion.

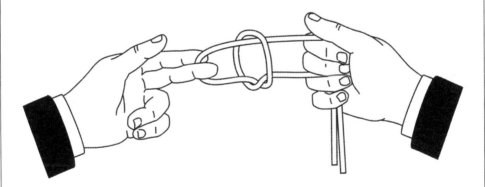

Rope preparation tip

Another alternative for "fixing" the ends of a piece of rope is to dip them in molten wax. Unlike glue this will dry and harden in a few minutes.

6

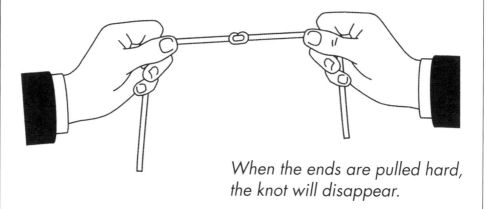

When the ends are pulled hard, the knot will disappear.

The Indian rope trick

In reports of this effect an Indian street magician (fakir) throws a long coil of rope into the air where it remains vertically rigid. A boy climbs to the top and promptly vanishes. The magician follows the boy to the top of the rope carrying a large knife and vanishes as well. The boy's severed limbs fall from the sky and are collected in a basket by the magician upon his return. Finally, the boy emerges unharmed from the basket.
So few people can lay claim to having seen this trick performed that it is generally considered to be a myth. Various magicians have managed to replicate the effect on stage, but as yet no one has performed the trick successfully in the open air.

Effect *A knot appears in the centre of a length of rope with a finger ring tied in it!*

Requirements *A piece of rope and a finger ring.*

Preparation *Thread the ring on to the rope. Hold the rope in your right hand with the ring concealed in your fist (illustration 1).*

● ●

1

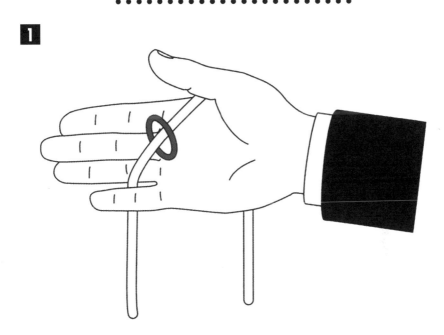

Top tips for tricksters

The quickest way to "fix" the ends of rope to prevent fraying is to wrap them with white or clear sticky tape. However, this is not suitable for some tricks in this book where the ends are switched for a cut piece of rope.

2

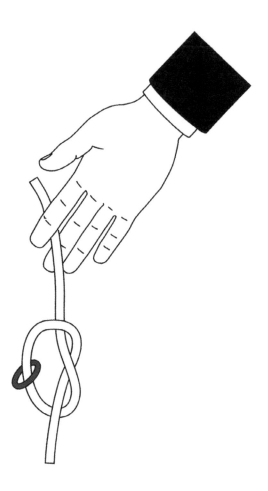

1 Perform "Another One-handed Knot" with the ring in position (illustration 2).

2 Keep the ring concealed with the back of your hand as you make the knot. It will appear tied on the centre of the rope when the knot appears (illustration 3).

To make this an even more impressive effect you could borrow a ring from a member of the audience and make it vanish earlier in your performance. When you come to perform this effect, you could secretly slide the ring on to the end of the rope under cover of your other "props" on the table.

Of course you do not have to make a finger ring appear in the knot – you are only limited by your imagination and the size of your hands!

3

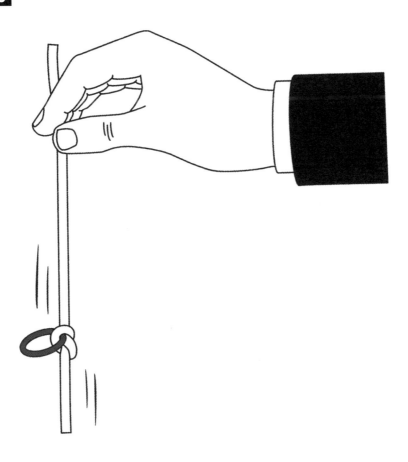

Effect *The magician throws a borrowed bangle into a knot.*

Requirements *A length of rope and a bangle borrowed from a member of the audience.*

Preparation *None.*

● ●

1

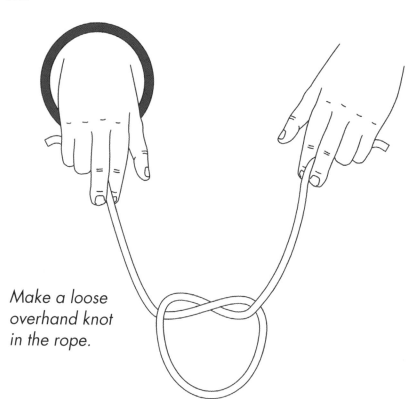

Make a loose overhand knot in the rope.

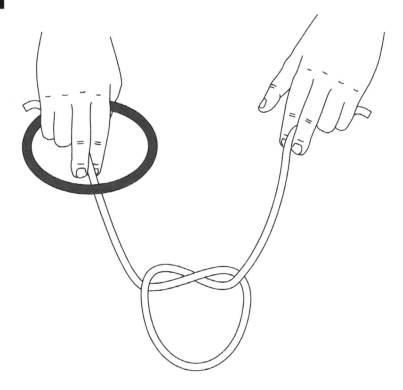

This trick will require quite a bit of practice before you acquire the necessary "knack" to be able to do it successfully every time. But when you become proficient, it is a very impressive trick which you can do at any time with a borrowed bangle.

Top tips for tricksters

Rope magic is very visual and is often featured in the stage shows of the world's most famous magicians. Many tricks in this book are suitable for you to perform to a large audience.

1 Tie a loose overhand knot in the centre of the rope. Put the bangle on your right wrist. Hold the ends of the rope between the first and second fingers of each hand (illustration 1).

2 Slip the bangle over the hand on to the rope. At the same time the right thumb clips the rope to prevent the bangle from sliding down (illustration 2).

3

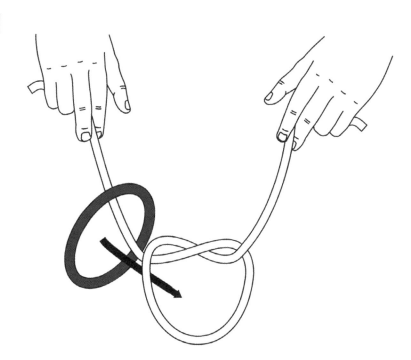

Top tips for tricksters

To make your rope magic more visible to the audience try to hold the props at your chest level. This also encourages you to keep your head up and make eye contact with the audience.

3 The right hand throws the bangle through the loop of the knot (illustrations 3 and 4).

4 When the bangle is through, pull the knot tight. The bangle appears tied in the knot at the centre of the rope.

What actually happens is that the original overhand knot melts away and a new knot forms itself around the bangle. It is even more amazing in slow motion than it is at true speed!

When you are really confident with this trick you might feel prepared to do it with a borrowed watch!

4

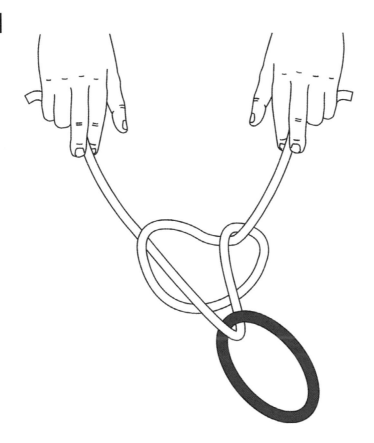

Effect *Three knots magically appear on a rope.*

Requirements *A rope about 65cm/25in long.*

Preparation *Tie a knot about 8cm/3in from each end (illustration 1).*

• •

1 Hold the rope as in the Quick Knot (page 196) with the knots concealed in your hands (illustration 1). The backs of your hands are towards the audience.

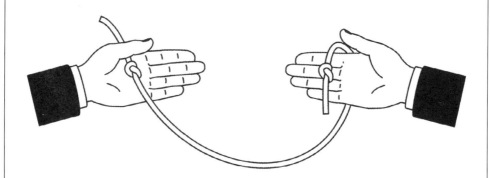

2

Pull

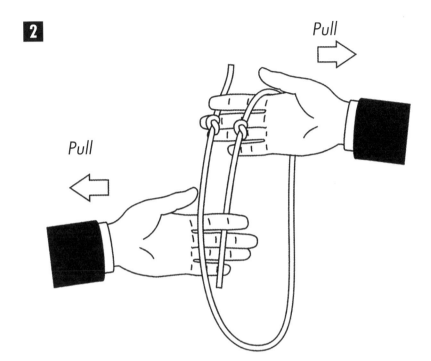

2 Perform the Quick Knot as described (illustration 2).

3 The Quick Knot will appear in the centre and the two end knots will now be seen (illustration 3).

4 All the knots seem to have appeared at the same time!

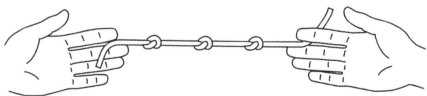

Effect *The audience watch the magician tie a genuine knot in a piece of rope. The magician then slides the knot along the rope and it comes off the end! The audience can keep the knot as a souvenir!*

Requirements *A long length of rope and a short piece of rope tied into a knot.*

Preparation *Place the knot in a pocket on your right side. Tie a slip knot (see page 192) in one end of the rope (we will call this end A). Hold end A in your left hand keeping the knot concealed (illustrations 1 and 2).*

● ●

1

A

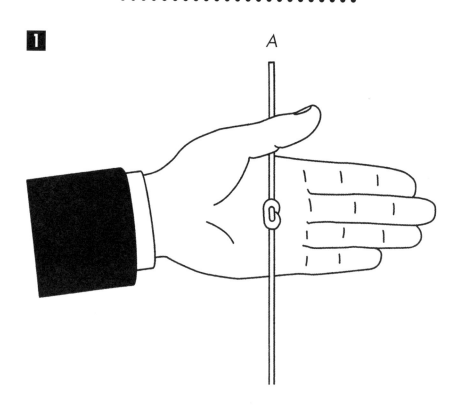

2

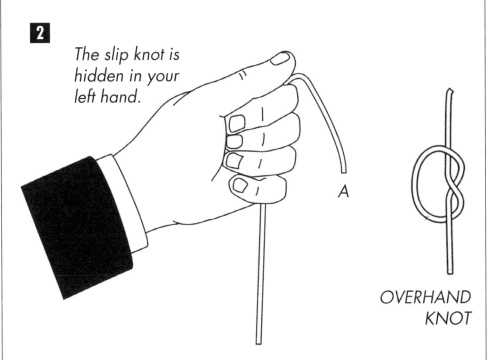

The slip knot is hidden in your left hand.

A

OVERHAND KNOT

1 Tie an overhand knot (see Glossary, page 192) in the centre of the rope, keeping the slip knot concealed in your left hand (illustration 3).

2 Hold your right hand just above the genuine knot with end A dangling down (illustration 4). Your left hand, still holding the slip knot, moves up to the genuine knot, apparently to slide it down the rope.

Top tips for tricksters

Remember not to use white rope when you are wearing a white shirt or jacket. If you must wear white, make sure you use coloured rope so that the audience can see the props!

3 But in fact your right hand covers the genuine knot as your left hand slides down the rope towards end A (illustration 5). Open the left hand to show the slip knot. The audience will believe this to be the genuine knot.

4 Now move the left hand and end A to the top, keeping the right hand over the genuine knot. Reverse the action in stage 3, moving the right hand up to the slip knot (taking the genuine knot with it) and apparently sliding the knot back to the centre.

 Slip knot is concealed in your left hand.

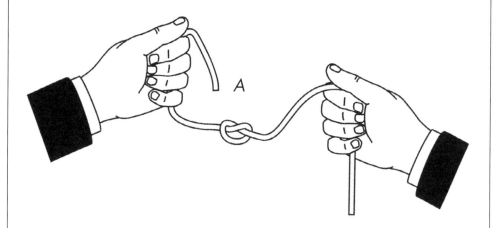

A

Top tips for tricksters

As rope is very inexpensive it is always a good idea to finish your routine by passing your piece of rope out to the audience to keep as a souvenir.

4

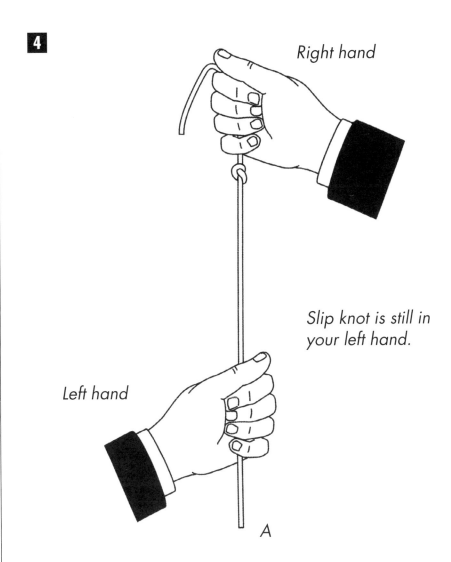

Right hand

Slip knot is still in
your left hand.

Left hand

A

5 While the right hand covers the slip knot, tug on the rope with
the left hand to "vanish" the slip knot. At the same time slide the
right hand to the centre. Remove the right hand to show the knot
is back where it began – in the centre.

6 You can have the rope and knot examined at this stage. While the audience are doing this, slip your right hand into your pocket and secretly take hold of the loose knot.

7 As you take back the rope, secretly slip the second and third fingers of your left hand into the loop of the genuine knot. Show the audience the knot in your hand.

5

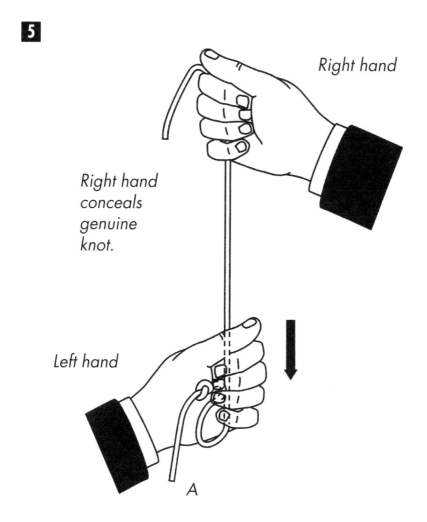

Right hand

Right hand
conceals
genuine
knot.

Left hand

A

Close your left hand into a fist, keeping the fingers towards you to conceal the loop of rope running over them (illustration 6).

8 With the right hand hold tightly to the rope coming out of the top of the fist and slide your left hand down. The knot will slide down the rope. Continue to the end of the rope, where the knot will untie. It looks as though you slide the knot right off the rope. Keep the left hand closed as though it still contains the genuine knot.

9 Bring the left and right hands together as though apparently passing the genuine knot from left to right. Throw the loose knot (which has been hidden in the right hand) out to your audience. This is a very powerful piece of magic!

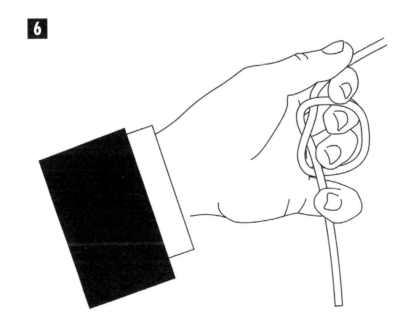

6

Effect *The magician throws a knot around a bangle dangling in the middle of a piece of rope.*

Requirements *A piece of stiff rope, at least 1cm/0.5in thick and about 150cm/5ft long, and a bangle (which can be borrowed).*

Preparation *Thread the bangle on to the rope.*

• •

1 Hold end A of the rope in your right hand and end B in your left, with the bangle dangling in the middle. Hold your right hand about 15cm/6in higher than your left.

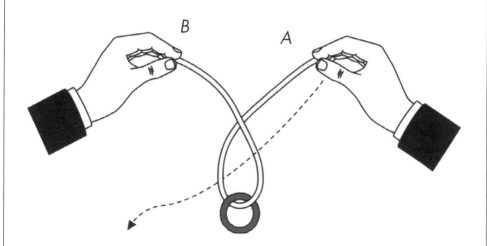

2

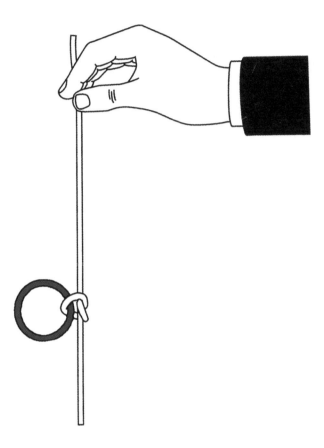

2 Move your right hand horizontally to the left and the left hand horizontally to the right so that end A passes in front of end B, and your arms are crossed over.

3 Now move your arms back to their original position. You will see that a loop forms momentarily in the centre of the rope. Act quickly. Throw end A through the loop to form a knot (illustration 1), and pull tight (illustration 2). This is a very impressive effect.

Effect *A loop of string escapes from a spectator's buttonhole.*

Requirements *A length of string 120cm/4ft long.*

Preparation *Tie the string into a loop with a tight knot.*

● ●

1

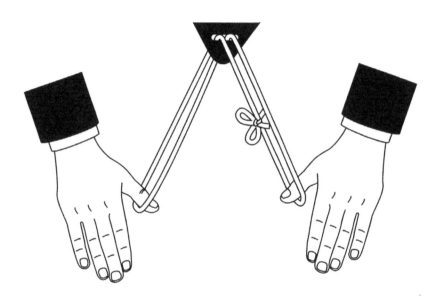

Top tips for tricksters

Remember that white rope can get dirty very quickly when you rehearse with it. Always try to use a fresh piece of rope for each performance.

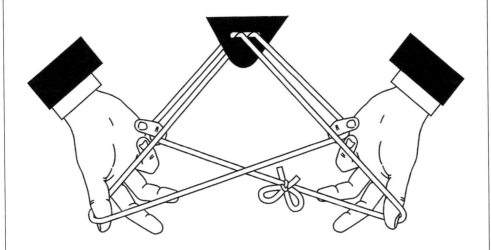

1 Thread the loop through the buttonhole of a spectator, and hook your thumbs through each end of the loop (illustration 1).

2 Bring your hands together. Insert the little fingers as shown in illustration 2 – each picks up the lower strand from the opposite side.

Top tips for tricksters

When using silk handkerchiefs in your rope magic always ensure that they are clean and ironed before each performance. Audiences DO notice.

3 Release the left little finger and the right thumb, at the same time pulling the loop tight. The loop will appear to pass through the buttonhole without damaging it (illustration 3).

Effect *The magician and a spectator are tied securely together, but they manage to escape by magic.*

Requirements *Two ropes, each 120cm/4ft long.*

Preparation *No preparation is required.*

• •

1 Tie one of the ropes around the wrists of the spectator (illustration 1).

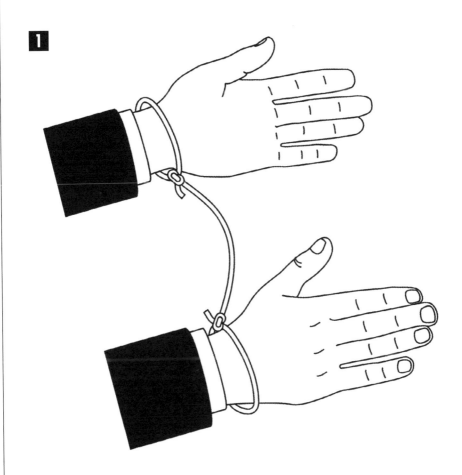

2

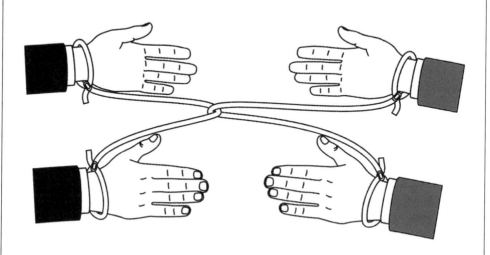

2 Have someone tie your wrists with the other rope, first threading it through the loop of the first rope (illustration 2). Explain that this is how convicts are transported around together, and it is thought to be very secure. However, it does not take into account the magical powers passed down to you by the Great Houdini!

Top tips for tricksters

Escapes are much more effective if you use the strongest-looking person in the room to tie the knots and make sure you are secure.

3 It seems impossible for you to escape, but it can be done. Pull the centre loop A of the spectator's rope and thread it under the loop tied around your left wrist. When you have enough rope pulled through, pull it over your left hand (illustration 3).

4 If the spectator now steps back you will both be free! With practice you can learn to do step 3 in just a few seconds.

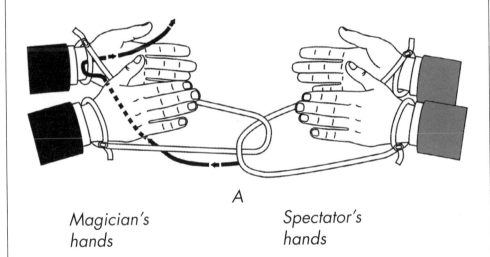

3

A

Magician's hands

Spectator's hands

Top tips for tricksters

Your rope will stay cleaner and whiter longer if you ensure your hands and nails are kept clean before practice sessions, rehearsals and performances.

Effect *A string is threaded through a straw. The straw is cut in half, but the string is unharmed!*

Requirements *A length of string, a pair of scissors and a straw.*

Preparation *Cut a slit about 2.5cm/1in long in one side at the middle of the straw (illustration 1).*

• •

1 Thread the string through the straw (you can fix the end to a needle to make it easier to thread it through). Make sure that there is an end of string dangling from each end of the straw (illustration 2).

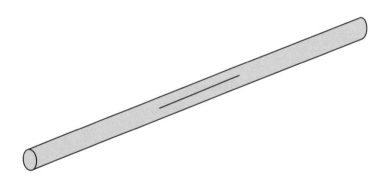

Top tips for tricksters

One of the most important rules in magic is to act naturally. Audiences tend to get suspicious when they see awkward or unnatural actions.

2

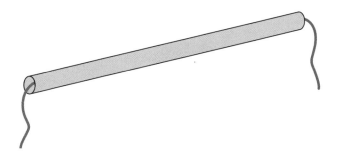

Explain that the straw is to prevent any possible sleight of hand. If the string is trapped inside the straw, when you cut the straw the string must be cut too. To make everything even more fair and above board, you explain that you are going to allow a member of the audience to make the actual cut through the straw.

3

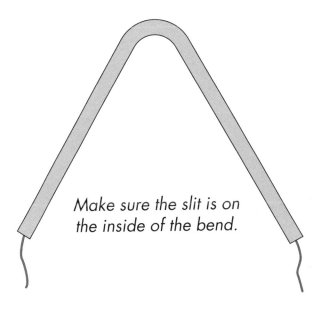

Make sure the slit is on the inside of the bend.

4

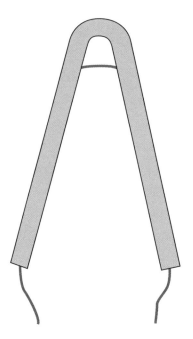

2 Bend the straw in half to mark the centre point where the spectator is going to cut (illustration 3).

3 Pull down on the ends of the string so that the middle of the string is pulled through the slit in the straw (illustration 4). This move should be covered by your hand.

Top tips for tricksters

Your family and close friends are often the hardest to fool. This is because they can spot when you are doing something unnatural.

4 Hold the straw so that the audience cannot see the "free" string. Get the spectator to cut the straw at the bend, making sure they cut above the string.

5 Even though it seems that you set up an impossible situation – the string was cut while isolated inside the straw – when you draw the two halves of the straw apart the string is undamaged!

5 *Make sure the slit is on the inside of the bend.*

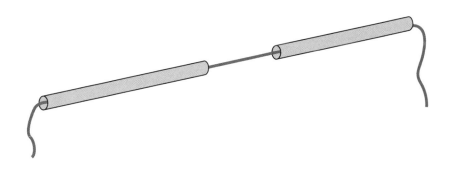

Erdenac

The French magician Erdenac has become famous among magicians all over the world for his performance of the classic effects of rope magic. He performs an entire act of rope magic with just a few pieces of rope, working silently to a musical background. He features the Cut and Restored Rope and the Unequal Ropes and concludes with Stretching the Rope. His act is titled "A Symphony with a Single Cord".

Effect *A member of the audience cuts a piece of string in half. When a borrowed finger ring is passed over the ends of string they melt back together.*

Requirements *A length of string, a pair of scissors, some rubber cement glue and a borrowed finger ring.*

Preparation *Pull apart and unravel the threads at the centre of the string (illustration 1). Pull out the unravelled threads (C) and twist them to make what looks like an end of string. Do the same with the threads (D). C and D now look like two ends of string (illustration 2).*

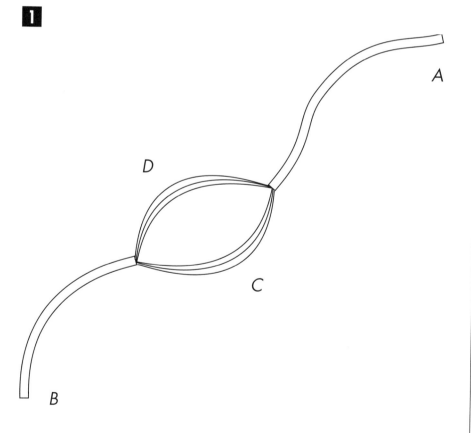

2

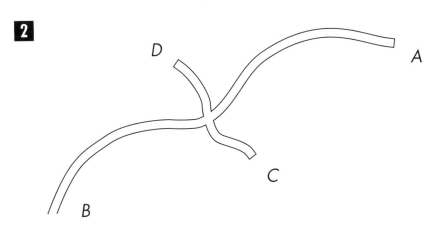

Hold the string as shown in illustration 3 with your thumb covering the join. You will appear to have two completely separate pieces of string. Nobody will suspect they are joined together.

Now glue the two real ends A and B together with rubber cement glue to make a loop.

3

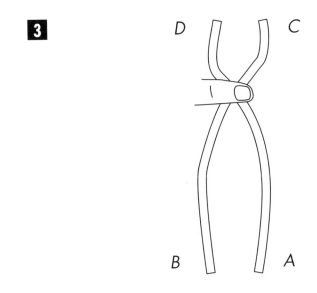

4

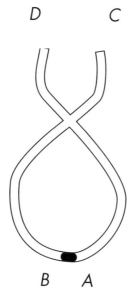

D   C

B   A

With your thumb over the join you appear to have a single piece of string folded in half (illustration 4).

• •

1 Display the string with your thumb over the join to show what appears to be a single folded piece of string. Hand someone the pair of scissors and ask them cut through the middle of the string.

2 Have two spectators each hold one of the ends just cut. Keep a tight hold of the pretend ends in the middle. Borrow a finger ring and thread it onto one of the cut ends (illustration 5).

3 After a build up, ask the two spectators to pull on their ends. Release your hold on the middle (illustration 6).

5

Magician's hand

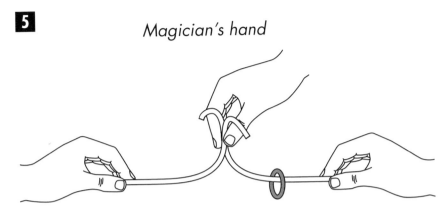

Spectator's hand

4 The ring will slide to the middle. But instead of falling off the end, it appears to pass over both ends and meld them together!

This is a very powerful illusion which will have a big impact on the spectators holding the ends. They are expecting the string to droop and the ring to drop on the floor. But instead they end up feeling the other spectator tugging on the other end of a piece of string that has been magically made whole!

6

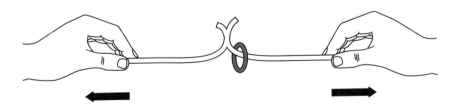

Effect *The magician releases a solid bangle from a length of rope.*

Requirements *A large ring or bangle (the trick is much more effective if this is borrowed from a member of the audience), a length of soft rope or string about 1m/3ft long and a headscarf or large handkerchief to cover the "mystery".*

Preparation *No preparation is required.*

• •

1 The way the bangle is knotted on to the rope is very important. Fold the rope in half and thread the loop through the middle of the bangle (illustration 1).

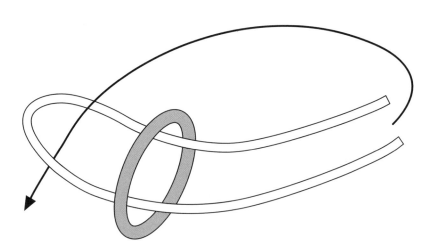

2

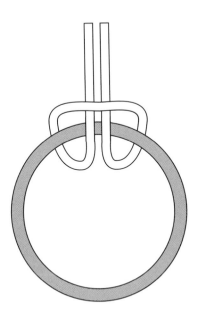

Explain that you would like two members of the audience to assist you – to ensure there is no cheating. You can say, "This is a mystery hundreds of years old that has been witnessed by the crowned heads of Europe, the mandarins of China and the small boy next door. It truly is a miracle."

2 Pass the two ends of the rope through the loop (illustration 1). Pull the knot tight (illustration 2). Ask a spectator to hold on to the two ends. Tell your audience that you have a hole in your

Top tips for tricksters

Magic can be very powerful when performed correctly. An audience which has been fooled will credit you with special power and skills.

3

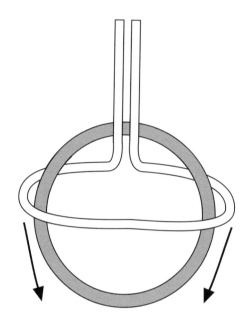

pocket. Reach into your pocket, as if to remove something, but don't take anything out – just hold your hand out flat and ask if they know what you have in your hand. They will, of course, say no. You tell them it is the hole from your pocket. Explain that holes are useful things if you are a magician doing tricks with bangles and bits of rope.

3 Cover the bangle with the headscarf.

4 Under cover, slide the loop around the outside of the bangle. This releases the bangle from the special knot (illustration 3). Say you are going to put the hole from your pocket in the rope to remove the bangle. Obviously, they don't believe you – until you remove the bangle!

5 Hand the bangle back to the person you borrowed it from to show it is unharmed. Mime replacing the hole from the rope in your pocket. Now the rope can be examined too!

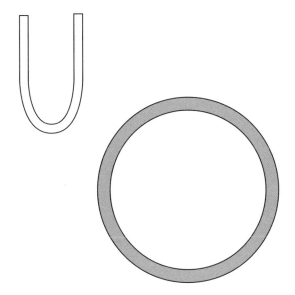

John Booth

Booth is one of magic's most respected magical historians and writers. He was also one of the first people to shoot "travel documentaries" for television and the lecture circuit. He has travelled to India on many occasions in search of the famed Indian Rope Trick – even going so far as to place advertisements in the major Indian newspapers – but, to date, he is still waiting to see it performed in its traditional form!

Effect *A knot vanishes, even though it is trapped on a knotted loop of rope.*

Requirements *A length of rope at least 60cm/2ft.*

Preparation *None.*

• •

1 Ask a spectator to tie a single overhand knot in the centre of the rope (illustration 1).

2 Ask another spectator to tie the ends of the rope together with as many knots as they wish (illustration 2).

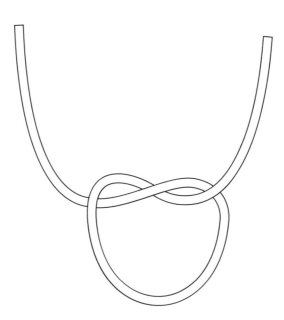

2

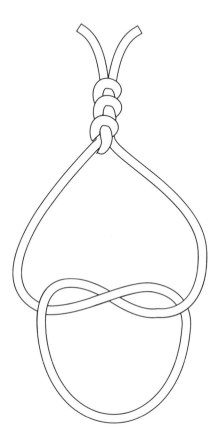

3 Point out that it is now impossible for the first knot to escape as you cannot undo it with the rope ends tied together. Explain that if a bangle or a ring is threaded on to a rope you only need one

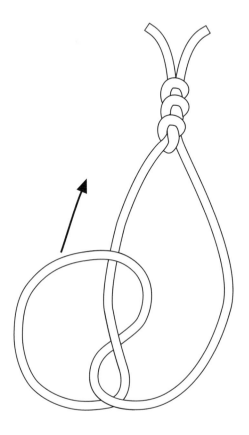

end of the rope free to be able to remove it, but to remove
a knot you need both ends free. So it is now impossible for you
to untie the overhand knot because of all the other knots the
spectator has tied in the rope. Surely it must be impossible for
anyone to untie that captive knot.

Top tips for tricksters

The hardest people to fool are children. The easiest
are a group of scientists or learned investigators.

4 Say that you are going to attempt it anyway. Place the rope behind your back and slide the overhand knot up to join the multiple knots at the ends (illustration 3).

5 Bring the rope out from behind your back – the original knot will appear to have vanished (illustration 4)!

Effect *After looping a piece of string over his thumb, the magician tugs on the ends, and the string passes through the thumb.*

Requirements *A length of string about 60cm/2ft.*

Preparation *There is no secret preparation.*

• •

1

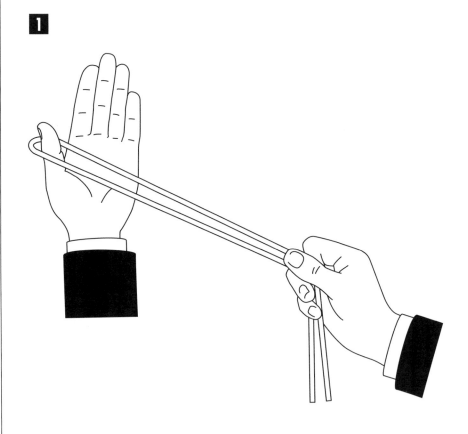

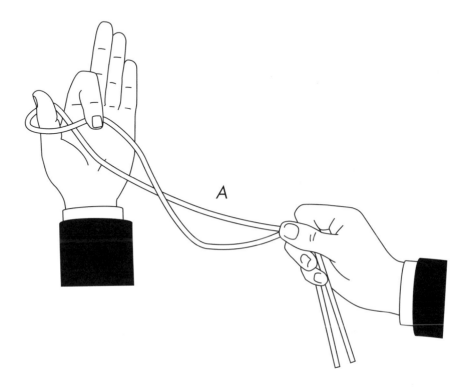

A

1 Fold the string in half and loop it over the left thumb. Hold the ends with the right hand, keeping the strands separated with the right thumb (illustration 1).

Top tips for tricksters

Travelling salespeople can use a few magic tricks to make a lasting impression on potential customers, and their existing clients will look forward to their visits!

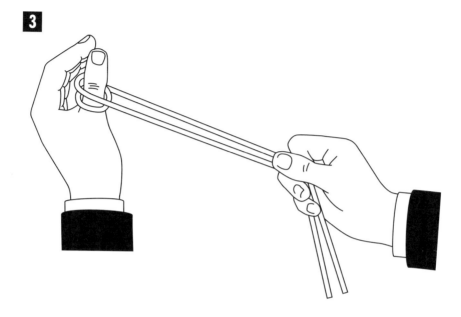

2 With your left first finger pull the front strand over the other strand and hold it clipped to your palm (illustration 2). Move the hands towards each other, and loop A over the left thumb, passing it round the back of the thumb to the front.

3 Twist the left hand around to the right and touch the tips of your left thumb and first finger.

4 Pull on the ends with the right hand and the string will appear to pass through the thumb (illustration 4).

Top tips for tricksters

Often you can change the props used in a trick slightly to help sell your business. One example is to use your business cards instead of regular playing cards.

4

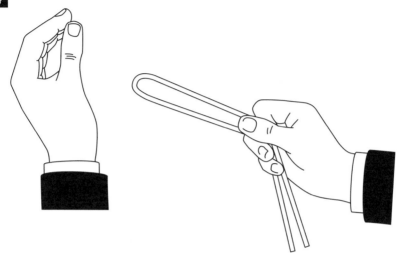

Effect *The magician makes a borrowed finger ring climb mysteriously up an elastic band!*

Requirements *A finger ring and an elastic band – both can be borrowed from the audience.*

Preparation *None.*

• •

1 Borrow a finger ring and elastic band from your audience if possible. Otherwise produce your own.

2 Stretch the elastic band between your hands. Secretly you stretch only the top half of the band – the slack is concealed in your left hand (illustration 2).

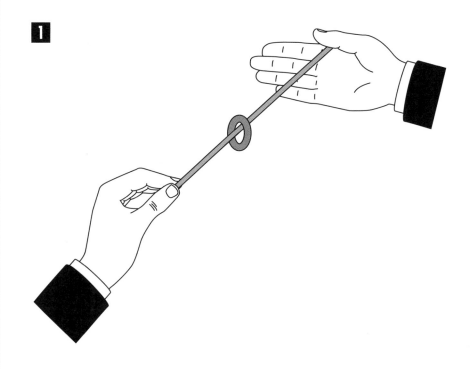

3 Ask someone to thread the ring on to the band. Allow the ring to drop down to your left hand and rest on the band. Stretch the top half of the band again.

4 Move your hands so that the band is at an angle of about 45 degrees, as in illustration 1.

5 Ask everyone to concentrate on the ring and see if they can get the ring to climb up the band.

6 Very, very slowly release some of the slack from your left hand. Because of friction, the ring will cling to the band and appear to be rising up the band.

7 Continue releasing the slack a little at a time until all the slack has gone and the ring has moved halfway up the band.

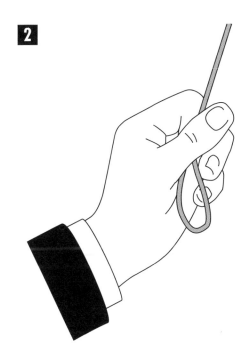

2

This is a very impressive effect which, when the necessary props can be borrowed, can be done impromptu.

You could write some patter to go with this trick to tie in with the Indian Rope Trick, saying that the ring represents the little Indian boy climbing to the top of the rope!

Effect *A rope appears to pass through the middle of the magician's assistant!*

Requirements *You need a length of strong rope about 3m/10ft long and a willing assistant.*

Preparation *You need to let your assistant in on the secret, as they do all the hard work!*

• •

1 Stand your assistant in the centre of your performing area. Make sure that nobody can see behind them.

2 You need two other volunteers to stand either side of your assistant. They will hold on to the ends of the ropes.

3 Get each of your volunteers to hold on to one end of the rope. Ask them to give it a good tug to make sure it is a genuine rope. Your assistant stands behind the rope so that the halfway point passes in front of their waist. Stand behind them and take each end of the rope from the volunteers to apparently cross them behind your assistant's back.

4 Your assistant holds their hands behind their back at waist level and points one thumb upwards, as in illustration 1. You don't cross the ropes behind your assistant's body – you hook them around their outstretched thumb (illustrations 1 and 2). Loop the right end over first, then the left end. Make sure the ends don't get twisted.

5 Cross the ends in front of your assistant and hand them back to the volunteers. Your assistant's thumb keeps the ropes taut. If they removed their thumb the rope would just fall away.

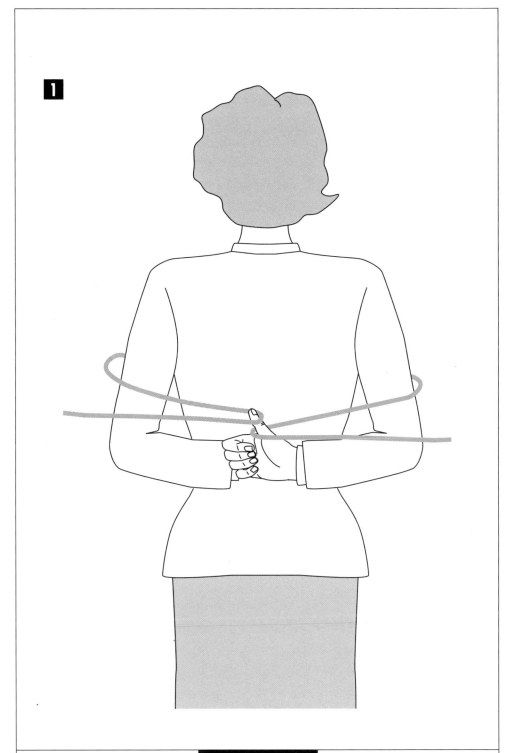

6 Explain that you are going to cut your assistant in two the same way cheese is cut! Get the audience to join in by counting down before the volunteers pull on the rope. When you say, "pull" your assistant removes their thumb from the loops in the rope. As your volunteers pull on the rope, it appears to pass magically straight through your assistant! Your audience can examine the rope – and your assistant – to see they are undamaged.

2

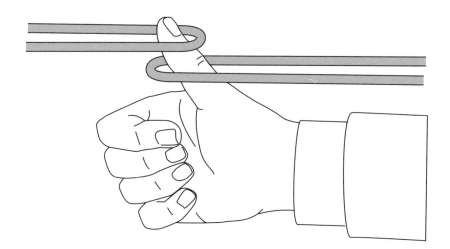

Notes

Notes